# No Time to Mourn

An anthology by South Sudanese Women

Edited by:
Hilda J. Twongyeirwe
Elizabeth Ashamu Deng

First published in 2020 by FEMRITE - Uganda Women Writers Association.

Distributed by African Books Collective

ISBN: 978-9970-480-17-3

Library of Congress Cataloging-in-Publication data will be available for this title.

Book Layout: Ronald Ssali
Cover Painting: © Abul Oyay
Cover design: Mutaz Hamed Mustafa

Any income from this publication will be used to support the work and activities of FEMRITE, a non-profit organisation dedicated to training, promoting and publishing African women writers.

To South Sudanese women and girls
across the universe

# Praise for *No Time to Mourn*

"These memories of home, these intimate conversations with sisters from South Sudan, are at once familiar and strange: the stories are raw and heart-breaking, the poetry is earnest and honest, the photography surprising and the art stunning."

Jennifer Nansubuga Makumbi, Author of *A Girl is a Body of Water*

"These are women's voices. They reflect the strength it takes to carry the burden of home – when home is etched in every cell of our being. No matter the circumstances, women always find themselves in each other's words and in each other's stories, as if it is one woman split in millions, living these lives and expressing these words with unimaginable compassion."

Ayak Chol, Author of *Once Upon an Obsession*

"The stories and poems in this anthology are intimate testimonies of South Sudanese women and children being abruptly and violently torn from home by wars not of their making or understanding. They feel like witness statements in a peace and reconciliation commission, each validating and amplifying the other. They are relentless in piling on the emotional horror, daring the reader to allow themselves to feel. What the women do not sacrifice is their dignity. Seeds of hope bear fruit in the stories of those who create new lives and livelihoods even from humble starts like selling groundnuts; and those who, against all odds, obtain an education."

Muthoni Garland, Founder of Storymoja Africa and author of *Tracking the Scent of My Mother*

"This moving and engaging book will leave you with a sense of renewed wonder and comfort in the knowledge that not only do such talented women exist, but they are also raising young girls, boys, women and men who will hopefully one day work for and enjoy life in a safer and more prosperous South Sudan. Ultimately, the book offers a genuine celebration of the women of South Sudan, by the women of South Sudan, for the people of South Sudan and beyond."

Awak Bior, Reading advocate and human rights lawyer

"This was a retreat of deep giving, by mentors and mentees. The result is soulful, moving and liberating. With these stories, the women move on to another page. I hope South Sudan too does. I know I want to read the next anthology from the same cohort."

Samuel Iga Zinunula, Ugandan Poet

The truths, the facts and the fiction, in *No Time to Mourn*, are so skilfully woven that they bring tears to our eyes.

Taban lo Liyong, author of *Another Nigger Dead*

# No Time to Mourn

# Table of Contents

## When Nowhere Has Felt Like Home

## Conflict of Identity

## The Peace We Yearn For

## My Sister's Keeper

# Editors' Note

In June 2019, FEMRITE and Oxfam collaborated to convene a week-long writing retreat for 18 South Sudanese women. The group, selected through an application process, included women living within South Sudan as well as those in the diaspora, specifically Sudan, Kenya, Uganda and Australia. The retreat aimed to give participants an opportunity to develop their writing skills, so that their voices and perspectives could contribute to public narratives of South Sudan—which are dominated by the opinions, analysis, and stories of male writers.

The retreat went beyond what any of us had imagined. The facilitators, including Ayak Chol Deng Alak, Lillian Aujo, Doreen Baingana, Harriet Anena, Mercy Ntangaare and Juliet Kushaba, helped plant seeds of affirmation among participants and at the same time encouraged them to reflect on their lives and consider, *What is the story I must tell?* It quickly became apparent that experiences of conflict, displacement, sexual violence and physical abuse had left deep trauma, and accounts of these experiences started to emerge. Writing and speaking provided an opportunity, that some had never had, to tell their stories. The women very quickly created a safe and supportive space to hold and support each other, counselling and comforting each other late into the night, forging a new sisterhood. Overall, six days together on the shores of Lake Victoria left us all with an even stronger conviction that the stories of South Sudanese needed to be heard far beyond the retreat space, because they represent stories of human experience in similar situations the world over.

Many pieces in the anthology were started during the writing retreat while others were selected based on an open call for submissions. The 41 women included in the anthology represent the diversity of South Sudanese women. They come from all regions of South Sudan. While some were born and raised within the country, others have spent most or all of their lives outside. For

many, the geography of their lives is split, between home and exile, punctuated by multiple departures and returns. With varying age ranges, their perspectives on South Sudan's political history are also diverse. Some have fought in war and some were born in war. Others carry the burden of war by virtue of the accounts of and impacts on friends and family.

No specific thematic guidance was given to the writers, but their poems and stories naturally coalesced around certain themes. In many pieces, writers express their deep frustration with traditional patriarchal gender norms that seem to impose themselves despite some writers' physical distance from South Sudan. The writers chafe against expectations of what it means to be a "good girl" or a "good wife." They reflect on the roles of their mothers and aunts, whose lives are consumed by domestic obligations, with conflicting feelings of admiration, gratitude, frustration and pity. With a few exceptions, fathers, uncles and husbands are absent, abusive or unfaithful. Scarred by war and lost in patriarchal predispositions, they are rarely capable of expressing love.

As South Sudan has been embroiled by war and violence for most of the past 65 years, war, death and destruction cast shadows over the lives of most South Sudanese. Some of the writers speak of direct, personal, raw, experiences in war. While others use allegory and minimalist writing, they convey rage, disappointment, fear, and loss; their pain is palpable.

Conflict has forced millions of South Sudanese to leave the country, and several writers narrate experiences of departure, rushed and in fear, without proper goodbyes. Living outside of South Sudan, the uncertainty of identity and of "home" that so many transplanted communities experience sets in. For the writers living in the diaspora, distance from South Sudan makes being South Sudanese confusing and frustrating. The writers vacillate between the desire to reclaim torn identity, thoughts of how to escape, disappointment at being pushed away, or fear of confronting that which they doubt.

Despite the pain and anger that colours most of the pieces, the resilience of South Sudanese women shines through. In challenging contexts, they still manage to feed their children, ensure their education, and even send money home to support those left behind. There is not a single piece where women just throw in the towel. The writers envision and demand a different South Sudan, one that is at peace, where there is gender equality, and where South Sudanese feel unity despite their diversity. For some writers, it is precisely the strength of women and their willingness to lift and support each other that fuels their dreams of a new South Sudan. Their hope is in the power of sisterhood.

Our hope is that this book, which is a collection of 18 short stories and memoirs, 48 poems, 21 artwork and photography pieces and one song, deepens readers' understanding of the experiences of South Sudanese women, that it drives the writers and artists included to continue writing, painting and publishing, and that it inspires more South Sudanese women to pick up their pens and brushes. There are so many stories that the world must hear.

*Hilda J. Twongyeirwe and Elizabeth Ashamu Deng*

# Foreword from Oxfam

Through this anthology of poems and short stories, readers are provided an opportunity to understand the impact of conflict on individual lives, on communities, and across generations. For many decades, conflict has been the norm for South Sudan. The depth of emotion expressed through the eyes, hearts and minds of these brave women writers should invoke in each of us a sense of urgency to do something: something about the long-running conflicts that have caused pain, trauma and dislocation of families and communities; something about the position and condition of women, many of whom experience the double jeopardy of falling victim to war as well as to violence in their own homes and communities, often justified by social norms and stereotypes; something about the promise of youth – wasted in senseless fighting; and something about the bitter legacy of the aged, lost in the anguish of combat and displacement.

Within and outside South Sudan, Oxfam is striving to build the resilience of South Sudanese while addressing the impacts of conflict. In South Sudan, we deliver humanitarian assistance, including clean water, hygiene facilities, food and income support. We help to make sure children do not miss out on education and we support people to rebuild livelihoods. We work closely with civil society to address discriminatory gender norms, to promote women's participation in peacebuilding, and to strengthen accountability of local and national government structures. Our programs in Uganda, Sudan and Ethiopia are responding to the situation of the over two million South Sudanese who have taken refuge in those countries. In meeting basic needs, supporting livelihoods, and ensuring safety, we strive to ensure that South Sudanese themselves participate and take leadership in addressing the challenges of their own communities. Committed to supporting durable solutions to the situation of refugees, we have worked to ensure that refugees have a place and voice in national peace processes, and we support refugee-led peacebuilding initiatives within camps and settlements.

This publication is part of our efforts to do *something more*—by providing voice to those who are rarely heard. Through a partnership with FEMRITE – Uganda Women Writers Association, we supported a process to bring together both seasoned and nascent South Sudanese female writers to think, foster belief in themselves, forge a sisterhood and share an artistic presentation of their thoughts and experiences – many of which were very personal, while others were fictitious but inspired by life experience. The result is truly remarkable.

My appreciation goes to each of the women who dedicated themselves to this project. I would also like to acknowledge the team at FEMRITE led by Hilda Twongyeirwe, for mentoring the women writers and for shaping and refining these artistic expressions we have today. Much appreciation goes to colleagues across the Oxfam confederation—from my team at Oxfam in Uganda, to Oxfam in South Sudan, Oxfam Ibis in Denmark, and our Horn, East and Central Africa regional office in Nairobi—for their support throughout the life of this project.

I believe that this publication will contribute to earnest dialogue aimed at resolving the distress of South Sudanese across the world, and inspire all those who may be battle-hardened, to find it within themselves to salvage the peace that the women, men, girls and boys of this young nation so desperately deserve.

Jane Ocaya-Irama
Oxfam in Uganda

# Introduction

## South Sudanese Literature Raised on African Writing Pickaback!

In 1965, whilst a third-year student in literature at Howard University, Washington D.C., I was so concerned about the place East Africans occupied in creative writing that I bemoaned it in an essay titled, "*How Can We Correct East African Literary Barrenness*?" This was in the East African Journal (EAJ) of May, in Nairobi. In literary circles, that essay came to be referred to simply as 'Literary Bareness.' By then, Sudanese writing in both Arabic and English was minimal. One of the few Sudanese who had published was Tayeb Salih from northern Sudan. The Northerners were Arabic language speakers, writers and readers, whereas Southerners were English users.

At the time, West Africa was coming up in all types of writing. The English colonies were sprouting short stories, poems, plays and drama, while the French speaking countries were sprouting poetry and satirical historical novels. Léopold Sédar Senghor of Senegal and Aimé Césaire of Martinique, the originators of the Negritude school of creativity, led in the field.

South Africa, where white settlers turned natives and citizens were living a creative life, was way ahead too in modern fictional creativity. They were writing in African languages—IsiZulu, IsiXhosa and SiSwati. Apartheid apart, education was advancing quickly in South Africa with missionaries largely responsible for the upsurge. Drum Magazine had helped nurture Johannesburg's Harlem Renaissance by providing a launching pad for a whole generation of writers and journalists, including Ezekiel Mphahlele, Lewis Nkosi, Nat Nakasa, and Can Themba.

When I returned to my continent, I went to Kenya to work in the University of Nairobi. Nairobi was the centre of urban culture in East Africa. In Uganda, Makerere University's English

Department was cultivating creative writing skills among students, supporting them to write and publish essays, poetry, stories and other works. The University raised up writers such as James Ngugi (as he was then called), Jonathan Kariara, John Ruganda, Elvania Zirimu, Peter Nazareth, John Nagenda and many others. Some of the students' works were, in 1965, collected into a "Pen Point" anthology called Origin East Africa, edited by David Cook. "Pen Point" was the English Department's creative writing magazine. The West Indian Nobel Laureate to be, V. S. Naipaul, was also invited to Makerere to be its Writer in Residence around the same time.

Indeed, after East African independence, the spread of universities helped spread literary creativity in East African metropoles. By the turn of the century, there was a lot of literary output in East Africa. Popular novels were coming easily from Meja Mwangi's pen. Ngugi wa Thiong'o was now producing volume after volume of books, in Kikuyu first and then English translations later. Ngugi's Weep Not, Child and The River Between came out of that period.

Writers from across the continent had influence on each other. When South Africa's Alan Paton's Cry the Beloved Country was published in 1948, it was followed by Lak Tar Miyo Ginyero Iwi Lobo (We Laugh to Show Our White Teeth), by Uganda's Okot p'Bitek, my friend, mentor and literary colleague. This was the first creative work in the Acholi language.

In South Sudan, we have had two major recent wars: The Anyanya War and the SPLM War. The Anyanya War of Liberation, 1955-1972 was a popular war with clear objectives and aims. Citizens participated in it voluntarily. It was against the Arab regime of Khartoum which had been formed by the sons and daughters of erstwhile enslavers. The Second War was the SPLM War of Liberation, 1983-2005.

When I returned to my land of birth in 1978, I joined the University of Juba and relocated with it when it was transferred to Khartoum. While there, a Dutch Ambassador interested in the gender discourse, Dr. Riet Turksma, engaged me to seek stories and folktales written by South Sudanese and published in magazines, journals and newspapers. She was after the fictive material rather than the factious, the formed rather than the found, which she judged reflects the truth of our lives. I am grappling with defining what I believe I achieved in one volume, in *After Troy*. This first anthology of Southern Sudanese writing included pieces by Agnes Lukudu, Victor Keri Wani, Dr. Francis Mading Deng, Moyigo Karokoto, Kaayi Spenser, Jacob Akol, Stephen Wondu, and Atem Yaak Atem. And so before we had a nation, we had a literature.

Now, in 2020, this anthology of short stories, poetry and art by a new generation of South Sudanese women is born. It is faction written like fiction. The facts of life these women have gone through are so expressively narrated that they come out so emotionally charged and read unbelievably true. The magical presentation of them does the transformation. We begin to think of them as imaginarily created. The major ingredient of fiction shines through the anthology. It affects us emotionally. Its truths can drive one to tears, more so when we realise that many of these pieces are first efforts by young women with very little formal training in producing a work of narrative art.

What has happened so that *Here, Chickens are not Vegetarian*, as stated in Nyakoda Joak Mundit's story in this anthology? Chickens have transformed from eaters of grains to relish flesh? Is it that chickens have turned to find out that the humans who relish chicken flesh could be eaten by chickens with equal return relish? What has happened that humans now do not care to inter their dead? Perhaps the chickens are rebuking the humans of nowadays, who kill themselves and leave their flesh to rot, and expect flies, dogs, birds and wild beasts to clear the result of their destruction? The casualness with which we now put men to death defies logic. The callousness with which we prohibit the bereaved from burying their dead is unbelievable.

The contributors write of the challenges of South Sudanese women and girls. The ups and downs of the girl- child's life in a traditional polygamous home and the life of a second or third wife in a polygamous house need to be experienced to be understood fully. In this anthology though, the writers convey the pains and frustrations for us all. Unfortunately, South Sudanese marriage practices, such as dowry payments or wife inheritance – where widows are taken up by their husband's brothers – trap women. After a husband has paid all dowry, the woman is enslaved to his home, regardless of if they beat the woman to-near-death, week after week. And like in many other African countries, there is no universal working social security scheme run by the government of South Sudan, with arrangements to take care of orphans and widows.

Perhaps the introduction of a universal social security system by the age-mates of these writers will do the trick, seeing that we, the BBC octogenarians have failed miserably in creating the South Sudan nation we had expected? Perhaps a Youth Political party of South Sudan will come, descending from Australia, America, Europe and England, leave alone Kenya, Uganda or Finland, to propose new codes of living and family raising and social protection? Things cannot continue the way they are reflected in *No Time to Mourn*. Going through the stories meticulously, one sees that we have enough people to draw a winning platform for reforming South Sudan.

I called this introduction: *"South Sudanese Literature Raised on African Writing Pickaback!,"* to put this anthology in the context of the development of the first generation of South African, West African and East African writings. The first South Sudanese generation of writings was composed of Ugandan-educated South Sudanese in exile as a result of the Anyanya War of Liberation of 1955 – 1972. Others were written by senior secondary school boys and girls and Makerere University students. Others came from Khartoum University graduates and extant students, the Juba

Commercial School graduates and students, Rumbek and Loka Secondary school graduates and extant students and the alumni, who were already working mostly as teachers or civil servants.

Here now, comes the second generation who have penned these short-story-like pieces from their life experiences under the tutelage of Hilda Twongyeirwe, on the FEMRITE sisterhood pickaback with support of Oxfam. My hope is that all of these writers will indeed become writers, rather than one-piece producers.

My call to the writers is to continue to write, share, and work, to master the creative writing skill. One of Nigeria's early writers, Cyprian Ekwensi, a pharmacist, learned writing by correspondence when he was selling drugs. Grace Ogot, the first Anglophone female Kenyan writer to be published, learned writing whilst working by correspondence as a nurse and later as an airline official.

Writers should therefore take advantage of every situation to make themselves better. They should frequent dramas and cinemas with the aim of studying how outlines are created and utilised by the writers, take writing classes, join writers' clubs, contribute to journals and magazines, join summer and weekend creative writing classes and attend literary talks. For if you were born to be a writer, you still need the language which makes you welcome amongst fellow writers. You need the technique of writing. You need to be familiar about fellow writers - present and past, of here and there. For we have no dictator among ourselves. Readers are not forced to read our books.

Above all, love doing things in groups. Take advantage of reading to audiences or in churches, submit your poems, stories, book chapters, to magazines and anthologies. Join a women's association and even a youth group with an experienced leader who has acquired the techniques of a coach, for a weekly get-together. Perhaps Hilda could design, with the assistance of her sisters, Dr. Susan Kiguli, Glaydah Namukasa, Gorreti Kyomuhendo and others, a two-week training for Writing Coaches and send them out with certificates and enough skills to train others and enable them write about the life dramas such as the current ones posed by the Coronavirus epidemic. They would have left testimonies of some of the darkest records in human life, in a time when we had thought we had mastered the world through science. Coronavirus, when it is over, those who will survive it after subjecting themselves to its vagaries, will have achieved a medal for survival. With such people around we know that humanity will be present.

Take advantage of COVID-19 and other lockdowns to create more. In the Black Death of the fifteenth century, Italians were in lockdown. What they are going through now is a repeat of the performance. Then a group of wealthy gentries went into the countryside campsite and they locked themselves in, telling stories in turn.

When I say I envy the editorial team, I hope they internally know why I do so. For it looks wonderful that these pieces all look so clean and polished, and that the writers seem to have accepted their honing painlessly. I think the editorial team nurtured these writers and their work and put their total hearts in it. The writers should thank them and wish them a long life.

Thank you Oxfam and FEMRITE for this unexpected present to South Sudan. In 1965, I had no idea that someday young women from South Sudan would surprise us with such a beautiful birth. I cannot cry about East African literary barrenness anymore! Even South Sudan has a literature.

May this child grow!

May it be followed by another child, and another, and another!

*Taban lo Liyong*
*University of Juba*

To Be Woman

# This is how to stay married
*Theresa Nyalony Gatwang*

This is how you cook
How you mix *akop*[1] flour
The favourite dish of South Sudanese
This is how you clean the kitchen after cooking
This is how you serve the food you have cooked
This is how you serve when you have visitors
This is how you ask your husband to eat
This is how you smile when there are visitors
This is how to hide your anger
This is how to stay married.


# The feminine principle
*Chudier Pelpel*

To be woman
is often misconstrued with position
or performance.
Her gender identity
is bound with her innate contributions
to the community she serves,
and the homes she carries.
She is
Daughter, Wife, Mother.

Fragmented and shared,
She omits her entirety

She
Thinks her transformations are not hers

---

1       South Sudanese dish, made with corn and wheat flour.

# Good girl from a good family

*Bigoa Chuol*

Here,
time is spent with little hands in soapy dish water
we know the nook and crannies of our family homes
more than we know our sensibilities

Here,
we are competent when we learn to subdue tiredness
to gobble unkindness like a delicacy

Before,
we know why we bleed
before we know what bleeds

Here,
we are in deep peril and consequently threatening to the virtues
of good men

Here,
we do not nurture our imagination more than young siblings
we boil tea for guests more times than books read
we brew binaries with cardamom and clove
we stay home even if it collapses and buries us
dead

Here,
we cannot extend warm conversation in language
but fortunately, can understand instruction

Before,
we strap down our breasts
and drape knees away

after we have been reprimanded to sit correctly
in the intermediary keep your eyes down
lest we know how to grow desire
and unhinge our jaws to open our mouths
to scorn reputation

Before,
we know we are perishables
that can blemish and spoil
should we keep close to deplorable friends

Here,
we stay dry and despondent
but always sitting correctly
at precisely the right angle
bending the wrist
still, little hands
in steady motion
cleaning
dusting
shrivelling inside.

# The almighty fist

*Veoulla Baker Ayul*

From the moment we were born, we were all taught the mighty ways to conform.

With our canvases empty and our eyes so pure, they painted us plenty and made us insecure.

Taking a backhand for rebellion against The Man.

Taught that we're fine as long as we keep ourselves in line. As we carry titanium on our fragile spine.

Tick-tock, got to watch the clock, we work 24 hours and our bodies never stop.

Aching, caving and breaking bone just to put some dollars in the pocket of the unknown.

# A poem for Mum

*Piath Noi*

My mother.
If one could carry the sum of her sacrifices
She would cradle hers in her arms.
Like a favourite child.
The one lovingly called upon,
Always relied on,
Celebrated for never letting her down,
Spoken highest of, for making her proud.
If sacrifice were a child
She would love him like the first of her 9.

It has been an unending journey;
For Loss has carried her far.
Taken her to places where nothing was for keeping,
Not even Number 6 –
Left divided between Heaven and Egypt's soil.
Still it paved a path through the desert, mothered her,
Used harsh lessons to teach her how,
Morphed into a boat to cross the rivers she cried,
Anchored her against the tides of oceans,
Grew wings into planes that carried her to places of taking.
Where many lost
And others displaced,
Found home.
Their lives yielding the misfortunes of giver and thief.

She was once a maid; she fed, cleaned and bathed to feed her own.
Never once mentioned the dangers she'd known
Leaving me to question if she truly left unscathed.
If one could carry the sum of her sacrifices
She would cradle hers in her arms.

*No Time to Mourn*

My Mother.
She would ask
"What is a broken heart if your back could still carry,
Your hands still work?"

Mother.
I could never give you the resilience that Loss had,
Teach you harsh lessons,
Pave a way in the desert.
Give and Take from you at once.
But I can be the child, the woman, the person
Who steps down from your shoulders
To thank you
for carrying me
for so long.

# Black fathers

*Chudier Pelpel*

Black fathers...
A stranger has forged his way into your home,
and your wives like mother birds have obliged because there are
mouths open in wait for food

Black fathers...
He has fixed the leaks with a band-aid because his arms are not as
strong as yours
but he is here and you've disappeared.

Black fathers...
He compliments your daughter's hair as he straightens out her
roots and gets rid of the coils
so that when she looks for a man it is no longer a reflection of
you.

Black fathers...
He has crippled your sons as they search for themselves in his
shadow
only to be lost in the abyss of his deception.

Black fathers...
They no longer sing about you,
But about the pain of your absence and their self-hate.

Black fathers...seeds are sprouting in the homes you left behind.

# The Phone Call

*Theresa Nyalony Gatwang*

The phone rang.

It was you.

The pain and wounds were fresh
I became weak and almost lost control
Can't even be master to my trembling hands.

I didn't want to pick up
I was tired of pleading
Of pushing against a permanent wall
Of trying to wake up something long dead.

My past was history.

I had settled.

Happy with my twins Nyadeng and Ayen
Raised without a father because you could not stand poverty
You moved on
You let go of my back
The surprise valentine present.

I let it ring
"My girls need no external drive from men of the land," I said.

But finally
You need to hear this:

Ayen is the new CEO of the World Bank
Nyadeng is one of the world's best journalists.

# Men who tremble

*Nyareeta Gach*

Men who tremble
with the thought of a woman in power
do not respect their Mothers.
Who taught you the sound,of M-
for /mämə/
before you called yourself
a Man
If you are threatened?

# Remarks at the Funeral

*Grace Akon*

The men are speaking for us again,
the way they always do.
Instead of eulogies
It is about how we should become more palatable women.

And I have not seen these faces in decades.
They only come to marry off a body for profit
or when the body ceases altogether,
They come to the funeral.

I do not have the hands to count
How many times the guests say
This grief will be good for me

Make me thinner, quieter.
They know my body has a habit of disappearing
when it wants to die.
They know women like me suffer quietly.

This would be sad if you were younger,
they make my brothers rise.
This would be sad if
nothing but weeping women were left of your father.

# Just because...

*Suzan Voga Duffee*

Just because she said it,
Doesn't mean she meant it.
Just because you saw it,
Doesn't mean it happened.
Just because you heard it,
Doesn't mean it's true.
Just because you touched it,
Doesn't mean it's real.
Just because you felt it,
Doesn't mean it lasts.
Leave her alone!
With me...
I'll say it and mean it.
You'll see it, it'll happen.
You'll hear it, it'll be true.
You'll touch it, it'll be real.
You'll feel it, it'll last.
Because I'm real,
What you see is what you get.

# Souvenirs

*Emmanuela Erasto*

Dear Love,

I hope these words find you in great health. As for me, I am doing fine. I am struggling to adapt to your absence and to those last words you flung at me as you left.

It's been two years since you left. Maybe this time it is for good although I do not seem to believe yet. You had been gone for many years but then you returned. People in the village said you were from Diaspora. I never cared about what they said. I knew deep down in my heart, you belonged here, where your umbilical cord is buried.

A few days ago, I went to Club 64 and sat in your favourite corner, or should I say our favourite corner. I am sure you remember it. While I sat there, my mind went back in time to those days when we would just sit there together for hours and hours without getting tired of the place or of each other. We would sip cups and cups of tea from the tea woman outside the club. She would boil big saucepans of tea which would be empty by evening. And do you remember the jokes and the laughter we shared as we sipped the tea? I remember the serious, yet very romantic fights we had too. Sometimes over very trivial things. We would sulk at each other but then quickly forget what it was we were sulking about. It was beautiful. We laughed. We loved.

Today life is different without you. In fact, so different, I sometimes can't recognize myself! Yeah! A bit harder and crueler too. Tastelessness has become my routine. I wish I could rewind the time, so it all becomes Club 64 all over again.

And do you remember Nyakuron Cultural Centre? I am sure you do. And the sunny days when we usually met there?

At first, no one at Nyakuron Centre knew where you had come from. See, you left the village when you were a small boy. But then you were a big man, asking someone's daughter for her hand in marriage. A big man with a face almost hidden behind a bush of a beard! When they asked me about you, I kept quiet. I never told them who you were. They wondered how all those things between us had started. But I did not care. You were described as that tall man with a black beard. Others described you as the tall man with a fake smile. It did not matter to me where you came from, how tall you were, or which smile you wore. You always said, "My fake smile is for fake people." Fake or not, it did not matter. It was from someone my soul loved.

You were 24 years old, Jamal, when we met the very first time. You loved my name. "Jamal and Jambala fit so well," you said. We talked that first day and before we knew it, we were making plans to meet again. More meetings followed and clearly, we had fallen in love. "I will crown you my queen," you had promised. I believed you, because when you said it and held my hands together, it felt like you were handing me the truth, and I held tight. From then on, we loved till the Nyakuron Centre crowd called me Diaspora Queen.

They all wondered what you had given me. I had always been a girl on my own. Suddenly it was Jamal and Jambala. I don't know what they think or say these days.

Three months later, you were nowhere to be found in Nyakuron. There were no more calls too. A wall of nothingness stood between us. Then you appeared that once. But you disappeared again.

Maybe I said something that upset you, that time when we last met? But what could I have said that you did not expect? It was a windy, Monday evening. We met at Nyakuron Culture Centre again. I sat to sip a cup of tea and nibble at samosas stuffed with meat as I waited for you. I noticed I was losing my taste for meat, but there was nothing else I could eat.

When you walked in, my heartbeat became irregular. I did not wait for you to sit down before I blurted out the words, "Finally we won the award of being together forever. See, I will be mother of your child soon. I am so proud of us." Words tumbled past my lips. You were quiet. "Hey! I have missed you." I said, trying to break your blank stare. You were staring like you had never seen me before. And you were silent. My heart was pounding in my chest, panicked about what could possibly be going on in your head. "I have missed you," I said again.

"Hey," you responded matter-of-factly.

"I am happy that you have finally come to meet me. I missed you so much."

"I have missed you too. So, what was the hullabaloo about me not coming to see you? Whoever I meet tells me you've been asking after me."

"That's not true. I have only spoken to a few friends. Your friends. Because I wanted them to tell you that I wanted you."

"Anyway, I am here now."

"Thank you. But why are you in a bad mood? I have waited for this moment. For you. For us to talk."

"Hmm?"

"Yes. And you stayed away longer than you had mentioned. Did you get a problem?

"Is that why you wanted me?"

"No. Not quite."

"You can tell me what you wanted then. I am here."

"You have not answered my question."

"What question?"

"You did not hear what I said?

"Oh, that. No. Nothing happened. I have been busy. That is why I took longer."

"By the way, you had promised you would call in case of delays."

"I have already told you I was busy. That is why I did not call you. But we can now talk. What was it you wanted?"

My heart raced. I had not prepared myself for this kind of confrontation. I opened my mouth and closed it again. Those days when I was quiet, you would encourage me to speak. You would finish my statements before they came out of my mouth, and your words were like mine. You were the first person to tell me the word soulmate. You said we were soulmates. That it is soulmates who think alike at the same time. And I believed you. I wanted to be your soulmate.

That day was different. You stood and stared at me like I was a useless tree or an insignificant stone at the roadside. I was not sure whether I should tell you why I had wanted to see you. Clearly, you were not the same man who I had last seen a few months back. You were different.

But I had no choice. Then, I felt like I had no choice. Finally I said it.

"You are going to be a father," I said.

"By the way, I called you, but your phone was off."

"We will have a baby in a few months."

"My work is so tiring of late."

"This doesn't make sense."

"What doesn't make sense?"

"I am telling you that you are going to be a father and that we will have a baby in a few months to come and you are telling me that you called and my phone was off? What is the connection?"

"Because I am not going to be a father and that kind of joke is not a good idea!"

"Would you joke with such news?"

"I know. So why are you doing it?"

"Because I am not joking."

"A baby is a bad joke. That is what I just said. And I hate bad jokes. For all the months we were together, you should know I hate bad jokes."

You said all the months we were together. I took note of your word: were. It had not occurred to me that we were not together anymore.

"From now on, just know it is not a joke."

*No Time to Mourn*

"So may I go now since you are bent on not communicating? And let's get this clear; I am not a father and I am not going to be a father any time soon."

"Do you really think you aren't the father of my child?"

"I don't just think so. I know so."

"Who then is, my dearest Jamal? Who else would be the father of my child?"

"I do not care. If you are carrying a baby, you know what to do. I am not responsible, and I want nothing to do with it. You can get rid of it if you want."

"Get rid of what!" I exclaimed in disbelief. "Are you suggesting that I should abort my child? Our child."

You did not answer. You saw me sit stunned by your words, my mouth wide-open and my feet trembling. You, my lover, Jamal, sat across the table, busy with your hands inside your trouser pockets. You looked strange. I had never seen anyone sit with their hands in their pockets.

"This is your baby Jamal," I said looking at the bump on my stomach.

"It isn't mine and I don't care who the father is. It is totally not my business," you said. The disdain in your voice shocked me. When you saw the tears flowing on my cheeks, you said you were sorry. Whether or not you apologised, it did not matter because I had already paid the price. Your sharp words had already sliced though my heart and my womb. Maybe that is where our baby got this thing from. And then you got up and walked away. You walked away, Jamal. You did.

You said I was causing a scene you did not want to be a part of. You walked away like my words had had no impact on you at all. Like the exchange between us that afternoon had not happened.

Tell me, were you afraid of me? Of us? Of being a father? Did you not care at all for the times we had been together? Did it cross your mind the kind of predicament you were leaving me in? My mother had always told me how our dad spoilt her when she was pregnant with her first child. How he would bring her roasted meat from the market. How she would ask for anything and receive it. Was I too naïve? But no. I cannot blame myself. Your camouflage was excellent, Jamal.

After you left me at Nyakuron, the waiter who we both loved came over to me. "Are you okay?" he asked me. I told him I was okay. He cleared the table and took away your cup. It was still clean because you never took the time to pour yourself tea.

It felt like a ritual. Like he was cleansing me of you. My cup stayed in front of me. I dried my eyes and sipped my tea. With each sip, I swallowed the pieces of pain you had served me. Each piece more bitter than the last. Your souvenirs. By the time I put the empty cup down, I was done with you. I told myself that I was not going to stay in the dark pit you had flung me into. But I cannot lie. I struggled. I struggled through everything. Fear. How would I raise a fatherless child? Shame. How would my family, friends and relatives receive my fatherless pregnancy? What answers would I give to the questions in the eyes of the villagers? Ruins. How was I going to pick up the pieces? What hope did I have?

For months I felt like a stranger in my parents' house. As soon as my mother saw the bump on my stomach, she asked me to go to my husband.

"You are unwanted in this house forever! How could you?" she said.

"I beg you mother, I am sorry. I will die if you send me away."

"It was your choice, neither I nor your father sent you to be a prostitute." Jamal, my mother called me a prostitute. For loving you. Up to now I sit and wonder whether that was your way of crowning me your queen. It is two years now. You have never called. You have never written. You have never returned.

After you left, I wanted to share my problem with my best friend Adya and also go to church and repent, but a voice in my head whispered: you do not need to speak to anyone or to repent. Carry your burden. It is yours. Why do you always run to Adya when you are in trouble? Isn't she the same person whom you have trusted before, who has let you down? Isn't she the one who always promises to keep your secrets, but always, after a while, mocks you in front of your peers? Do not go to church and do not go to Adya. If you go to Adya, she will tell everybody: Diaspora Queen is in trouble. Of course, you remember Adya, don't you? My best friend. You met her several times. Adya does not know that you came and left. She does not know who the father of my child is. Nobody knows, Jamal. Not even my parents. But I know people guess, probably. I am not blaming you of course. I am just saying.

I still have good memories of us, Jamal. They have never faded. Feelings are unstoppable, sometimes, but we have the power to direct them. That is why I can sit here, hold a pen and write this letter, smiling. My paternal Uncle gave our child a name – Wani.

By the way, do you have children? A wife? Do they know you had another life?

Do you want to know what happened to our baby?

Peace and Light,

Your Queen.

# Darkness in Kaku's Diary

*Juan Evalyn Mule*

Late one night, the moon shone bright above our mango tree and the stars were bright in the sky. Everyone in my home and in the neighbourhood was already in the world of fantasy. I loved sneaking outside when everybody was asleep. It felt like I had special powers and could do anything to anybody in the village without them knowing. Sometimes I imagined casting a spell on them so that they would not wake up in the morning. That would be the end of the whole village, I always thought. At such hours, it would only be the snoozing snores from different huts communicating with each other.

Mama told me to be careful with the night, but I did not fear. She had taught me early, that nothing could harm me in our compound. She used to come with us outside at night for a short call, but when I turned eight years and my sister was six, she stopped taking us.

"Go," she would say to us. "Nothing can harm you." She would stand at the door then we would go together and wait for each other near the pit latrine. It did not take long before my sister and I were relocated to another hut in the compound. The huts were close to each other. Mother would tell us that nothing could touch us, and we believed her.

Later when she started finding me outside alone, she would tell me to be careful, but I did not believe her. That was not the story she had engraved in my heart. So I would wait for her to close the door to the hut she shared with Baba and I would sneak outside again. I would stand in the compound and listen to the night or just stare at the sky and speak to the moon. Again it was mother who had taught us to always look out for the moon. She would then tell us to smile and make a wish on every new moon. We enjoyed our conversations with the moon.

As I stood outside, the night breeze pierced through my skin and I went back inside our grass thatched hut. I joined my sister on our papyrus bed in the middle of the room and willed my mind to sleep as I looked at the animal skins tied on the roof where Mama kept pieces of dry smoked meat that she would cook only when Baba came back. Baba always went away on journeys. The sweet aroma from right above my head always woke me up in the middle of the night. Then I would know it was time for a short call and I would go out. Sometimes I would call my sister. Sometimes she would sense my movements and wake up. Or maybe she too had her own body clock that woke her up.

But this night was different. I must have just slept as the sweet aroma had not yet woken me up and I had not gone out for my routine short call when I was woken up by a noise from our parents' hut.

"*Poni…Poni…Poni!*[2]"

It was Mama's voice. I could hear her scream, calling out for her dead mother. I knew at once that my father had returned from his trip unannounced.

"Please stop Baba Kaku," mother was saying but father was silent.

"*Poni…Poni…,*" mother continued.

I could hear things falling and breaking in their room as Mama continued to shout. She shouted at intervals as blows and punches rained down on her body. My beautiful mother was being beaten by the love of her life, Baba my beloved father. I was 10 years old and did not know how to stop father's rage. My sister was even younger. She was eight and fast asleep. She rarely heard them fight and every time I told her about the fights in the morning she would never understand because father would be unpacking his bags and giving us sweets from his journey. And he would be talking to Mama like they had had no fight at all.

---

2        Poni was the name of my dead grandmother. South Sudanese often appeal to parents or ancestors when in distress.

Mama was screaming really loud and all our neighbours were either asleep or pretending to be. No one came out of their huts to help her.

But then why did he treat her really well sometimes? Then she would be happy and say to us, Baba Kaku is a good man. We would believe her and giggle and be happy. We would run to father and jump over him or count his fingers and toes and tickle him. He would tickle us back. A good man. And then on nights when he hit her, we would be confused. Is our father a good man? Is he really our father? He himself always told us not to fight and not to hurt each other. We did not understand why he would fight and hurt mother. At first we thought that when big people fight they do not feel pain. But as we heard mother wail in pain every time father hit her, we knew that they too felt pain.

Mother was now wailing. "You are killing me Baba Kaku. You are killing me."

I shook my sister but she was fast asleep. I shook her again and again, but she did not wake up. That girl! Maybe that was why she always wet her bed. It was so hard for her to wake up once she slept. Even when I pinched her and pulled at her toes she would wince but not wake up. I sat on the bed and listened.

"You are killing me Baba Kaku," my mother was shouting.

"Let me kill you today, woman," Baba responded as he continued to hit her. "You cheat!"

"Help. Help." Mother's screams were becoming faint.

Fear gripped me. My legs and arms felt very weak. "Maybe she is dying this time," I said to myself. I could not ignore my mother's helpless cries anymore. I was at the climax of my patience. My heart was pounding and I could hear it, bu bu bu bu. I grabbed my torn sweater and put it on before I picked the *taija*[3] and matchbox. I stepped out of the hut and tiptoed to their hut. As usual, their door was locked from the inside. I banged it but my father did not yield. I waited outside the door. Father was known for his anger and what he could do if anybody interfered in what he called his family

3     African oil / paraffin lamp. It is made out of old tins.

business, even us. He had told us that children must never meddle in grown ups' issues because they cannot understand them. My body was shaking and my hands were trembling. The thought of losing my mother seemed a nightmare yet so real. I tried to steady my feet on the ground but the cold night wind, the darkness and my mother's wails could not allow me to be still. I shook and my teeth rattled. I moved round to the back of the hut. The broken windowpanes were held together with a bunch of ragged nylon clothes tied in several knots.

"Don't father! Don't! You will kill her," I shouted. He did not respond. All the while he continued to hit her. I moved away and ran to the pile of firewood where I fetched one log. I placed it against the wall so I could climb on it and reach the window. In no time my small feet and hands were hugging the log, climbing like a chameleon. It was father who had taught us how to climb by leaning logs against the surfaces we wanted to climb.

I pushed against one pane and it caved in. Inside, Mama was on the floor pleading with Baba to stop as he was stood in front of her. He was hitting her with his belt.

"Baba no! Please," I cried.

"Like mother, like daughter! Get out of there before I come for you," Baba roared thunderously. I felt as if my heart was popping out of my chest.

I slipped off the log and fell to the ground. I hit my nose on the ground and it burned. I felt as if it had expanded like a balloon and would explode any second. My eyes burned as though *piripiri*[4] had dropped into them. I breathed heavily. Contents of my stomach seemed to be boiling. Ngonga, mother's brown goat bleated. I was close to her shelter. Mother had bought Ngonga and named her after a series of beatings from Baba. "Ngonga," she had said to the goat. "Let's share this pain." And Ngonga, the goat had become, and remained.

"Father, stop!" I cried. I wished I could call the police but

---

4     Hot Pepper.

I couldn't. This was Kajokeji, not the Australia that my cousins had told me about where such fathers would be arrested and even jailed for assaulting their wives. But how would I call police? I had no phone. And if I had a phone and I called, would my father ever forgive me? I asked myself.

"Father, stop!" I wailed. He did not stop.

I struck the matchbox, lit the *taija* and made the sign of the cross. I put the tin on the roof of the hut and tongues of fire started to rise into the sky. It was only fire that could stop father from killing my mother. But she was still on the floor. "Mama! Mama! Mama" I called out.

I ran round the hut and met my father at the door.

"You fool, you have burnt your home!" he said. I did not respond. I ran past him but he grabbed me and cast me outside. He ran back to the hut and came back carrying my mother. He cast her on the ground. He ran back inside the hut and pulled out as many belongs as he could get all the while shouting, "Fire! Fire! Fire!" The neighbours who had been quiet surfaced and without being told what to do, they started helping father to put out the fire using whatever their hands landed on. I sat next to my mother and cried as everybody went on with the business of putting out the fire. Several minutes later one of the neighbours heard my sobs and came to where I squatted. He shone his small torch on us. Mama lay still. The black circle in her eyes had disappeared and she was not blinking. Blood was oozing out of her nose.

"Mama Kaku," the neighbour called.

"Yes," she whispered. I was shocked that she could hear and that she could speak.

"Mama!" I called her.

"Take me to hospital," she whispered.

My mother was alive.

I wept.

Mama spent days in the hospital. We would visit her every day and take her food. Then one day we saw her return accompanied by two policemen. She was still weak but she could walk.

"You have a case to answer," the policeman in front of her said to father who they found standing outside the hut.

"Me?"

"Yes, you. We have come for you."

"You can't possibly send me to jail," he addressed mother.

"No, she can't," the second policeman answered. "It is your inhuman behaviour that will send you to jail. But do not worry. We are taking you only for a few months or even days to help you taste pain. When you return and still fail to live with human beings, you will be locked up for life. I promise you that."

My mother lowered herself on the veranda and sat down as her husband was being led away.

# Memories

*Winnie Elijah Musomba*

I was young, my eyes glittering with passion for him. Mamuch was his name, very tall and dark unlike me who was short and light skinned. People called me Nyebony: ripe. He was the envy of his peers and mine. He had style, a very well-toned body that matched his set of milky white teeth with a gap in the middle. The girls always drooled over him. A military man with ranks, a commander of sorts. He was every girl's dream. But I did not care, I was the girl of his dreams.

The confessions from his calabash of love never ceased to melt my heart. It was filled with promises: promises of a grand dowry, beautiful children and a gorgeous home with a big farm filled with maize, cows to milk all day, and goats.

"I will make a big farm for you and my children. I never want to find you hungry," he would say to me.

I would smile and hold his hands and just stare at him.

In the evenings after helping my mother with the house chores, I would politely excuse myself and go meet Mamuch. My family loved him. He was from a good family and respected everyone equally. His qualities were so admirable. All my family members looked forward to the day we would tie the knot and say I do.

It was my aunt who sometimes teased me about him. She would smile and say that there is never a beauty without a fault. But there was no fault with Mamuch. There was never going to be any fault. It would be happy-ever-after for him and me.

By the stream in the beautiful land in Upper Nile, South Sudan, we would sit on the soft carpet of grass as we watched the scorching sun setting, giving room to the much needed cool evening breeze. The orange yolk rays of the sun were always breath-taking. This was always the perfect time to speak about our future. In those moments, his ranks did not matter. My ripe colour did not matter.

A few years into our relationship, fortune smiled upon us. Mamuch was chosen amongst those who were sponsored to travel to Cuba for studies. South Sudan was equipping her children with skills to enable them to contribute to the development of the country. I was very happy for him, for us, because I knew that his opportunities would broaden. He told me how he would think about me every day he would spend in Cuba. I promised I would live for him till he returned.

"This is the beginning of a bright future for us," he said to me.

A year passed, two years, three... and there was no mention of Mamuch's return. Four years, five. I still waited. People talked about him. They talked about us but I ignored them. People have a way of peeping into what does not concern them. I did not respond to their talk because my hopes for his return never grew thin at all. My love for him was constant, like he never left. I went to live with his sister in the big city of Addis Ababa. Being with his sister made me feel a bit close to Mamuch. Before he left for Cuba, we performed a ritual where I got engaged to him. In the ritual we took a promise to wait for each other. It was only fair that I moved in with his people, his family. Kuliny was kind to me. She prepared a room for me in her home. She provided all my needs and even took me to school to learn some English. She even went ahead and enrolled me in an institution where I learned hospitality skills. I was in a loving home, her children were very intelligent and welcoming. They made the weight of waiting lighter.

News of his return found me at his sister's place. It was a good five years of a long wait. It was finally over. I was all over the place like a new born calf, full of excitement, full of life and not sure of where to step. That day, I washed all my clothes and bought a few new ones. I rubbed my feet, cut my nails and went to the salon for a fresh look. My room was sparkling clean with the aroma of bakhoor, the best incense I had saved for months. I had got it from Mary, the house-help, when I asked her for advice on how to prepare for his arrival. She told me to be humble and receive him

*No Time to Mourn*

like I would a king. She gave me the incense and said it was the best for lovers. She was so nice to me. I called her Aunt Mary.

When the car carrying him arrived in his sister's compound, I did not know whether to wait until he got into the house or to run to him. Before I could decide, my legs betrayed me. I found myself walking towards him and in no time, I was sprinting. It was as if he was going to disappear or be whisked away before I reached him. As soon as he saw me, he disentangled himself from everybody and reached out to me. He gently gathered me into his arms and lifted me off my feet. My legs dangled in the air and I did not care who was looking. After all I was betrothed to him. He was mine and I was his. His grip was stronger and his body bigger than when I had last seen him. When he put me down I walked next to him as I stole glances at him. His height was even more intriguing, and he had a more mature look. A beard grew under his nostrils in a pyramid shape. A sweet smell wafted over his body. I would do anything to burry my nose under his clothes and just be there, smelling only him. My face started to heat up and just then, like the Nile, warm tears gushed down my cheeks. Like a new-born baby, I cried without stopping. Not even his gentle voice could comfort me and stop my whimpering.

Finally, I was in his arms again. For a moment I was transported and transfixed to the orange yolk rays of the setting sun of the Upper Nile. I was seated by the stream with Mamuch.

That evening I begged him to switch off the lights and he chuckled as he reached out to the switch.

"You are my woman. Are you still scared of me?"

"I am not, Mamuch," my heart was pounding as I said the words. I feared he could hear it.

I undressed in the pitch darkness and wondered why I had gone through so much trouble searching for head-turning inner wear.

I dived under the bedsheets and blanket. Mamuch laughed.

"Where are you my dearest? I can't see you," he said as he snuggled closer.

"Of course I am here," I responded.

It was my first time to sleep on the same bed with a man, let alone be with a man alone, in a room. I was as shy as a mouse, but he managed to keep me relaxed. He was very impressed that at the age of twenty-five I was still pure, for him.

"Thank you for waiting for me," he said in the morning as he covered my whole body with kisses.

"I hope you waited for me too," I said timidly.

"Of course you know I did. Do you doubt me?" he responded.

"But how would I know? But no, I do not doubt you."

"You sound sad."

"Because I cannot know whether you waited. Because women cannot know whether their men waited and yet without a doubt, men know whether or not their women waited." I had heard many stories at the institution where I had been studying hospitality skills. Blind trust was a difficult venture.

Mamuch silenced me by taking my lips into his. I submitted.

With my white bed sheet at hand, I ran to Mary that morning. Like a dog with two tails I showed her the evidence of my purity. She was the only person I could share personal matters with.

"I have always known you were a good girl," she said to me.

"Thank you, Aunt Mary," I said.

A few days later a party was arranged for Mamuch. All his close family, friends and neighbours attended. The big radio he brought with him from abroad put all the small radios to shame, with its bass and volume. I was glowing with joy. Everyone was happy; people were chatting and laughing. Food and drinks were plenty. Tall, dark-skinned, beautiful ladies were also plenty. That is where Mamuch's attention was for the whole time during the party. I couldn't help but notice how inappropriately he touched some of the women at the party. I consoled myself and tried to ignore the whole drama. I wasn't going to be a wet blanket on his day. As the red flags kept showing themselves, I just kept talking myself through it all, telling myself to play it cool. I trusted him since he was not drinking and had never been a drunkard. His judgment was not impaired.

That night I slept alone.

"I have to see off my friends," he said as he walked away with the last batch of young men and women at the party. He did not return and did not communicate. I worried the whole night. It was not clear to me where he had gone. I was awake till morning, wondering. I had no phone and so could not even call him. I respected his sister so much, I thought it would be uncouth or even shameful to wake her up and ask. After all, wasn't it my duty to know my husband's whereabouts? I expected him to give me an explanation when he came back home the next day, but all he said was that they decided to go out and complete the party. However, his eyes seemed to carry a different story, and they looked away to shield whatever it was.

From then on, a lot changed about him. He spoke less to me and would go off and return as he wanted. When I asked about whether we or him alone would return to Upper Nile for state duties he said it would not be soon.

"Five years away in Cuba changed a lot of things," he said. He still kept his uniforms, but he did not wear them.

"You are still in the army," I said.

"I am still an army man," he responded. In Addis Ababa, he lived a civilian life. I had hoped that maybe if we returned to Upper Nile where I had relatives, he would respect me more. He had really changed. I did not realize how much till the day he laid his hands on me. I never told anyone as it happened in the privacy of our room. But also, I was too shocked to talk about it. It felt like it had not happened, yet it had. Little did I know that it was going to become routine. When Kuliny travelled for a business trip it became worse. He accused me of taking contraceptives to avoid pregnancy, to avoid giving him children. I was no longer sure of my love for him as it was overshadowed by fear. I was angry all the time because *I bit my lips* about the abuse I was undergoing. Kuliny's children were young and couldn't intervene; Mary tried to help but she had no say in our family matters. I was petrified of reporting the incidents to Kuliny. I feared the beatings would get much worse if Mamuch found out that I reported him. I thought of reporting to my family, but what would they do anyway?

Infidelity crept in like the darkness of night, to a level where he laid his dirty laundry in full public view. I was mute to all of it. I once found on top of our bed, a bra belonging to one of his nieces who had come for a short visit. I had moved out briefly to the market. I knew it was Tabitha's bra because she was the only one in the house with such a huge bust. When I confronted her, she scoffed at me and snatched the shapeless bra out of my hands. She then turned and said she was only changing clothes from my room. The explanation did not add up considering that she had her own room. When I asked Mamuch about the incident, he gave me an even bigger blow. Not only did he beat me that night, he even chased me out of the room. While I slept on the couch in the living room and pretended to be asleep, I saw him take Tabitha to our room. I heard the key click in the door. I was dumb struck. With my own two naked eyes I saw Mamuch take Tabitha and lock the door behind them.

When he opened for her to come out towards morning I sat up and stared at the two of them. He saw me looking straight at him but he did not even twitch a muscle. A man who was capable of such a deed was capable of doing anything to me, I thought. At that point I decided in my heart that I was a widow. But I stayed. I do not know why I kept holding on to a man that no longer existed. I thought I could bring him back to life, back to loving me, to caring for me, and to fulfilling all the promises he had made to me. I tried, but the Mamuch I knew was dead and gone, buried in a graveyard of the unknown.

*No Time to Mourn*

After two agonizing years at Mamuch's mercy, God finally heard my prayer. Mamuch ran off with another woman. I was filled with relief, yet scared that one day he might return. I continued to stay with Kuliny as I was her worker now. I managed her estates including her home. She was a busy woman.

Just as I feared, one evening we were home and Mamuch walked in.

"I am sorry," he said. We talked the whole night and I believed him. People told me to give him a chance and I did. As it turned out nothing had changed about him. New issues emerged out of thin air. He accused me of looking good while he was away. He accused me of cheating on him. He became jealous of my responsibilities in Kuliny's estates. Kuliny had bought me a phone to help me coordinate my responsibilities. Mamuch accused me of using the phone to coordinate my sexual affairs. It did not take him long before he delved back into promiscuity and violence.

I decided it was my turn to run away. I was tired. I talked to Kuluny and she gave me a go-ahead.

"No one will blame you my sister," she said. "You have done your best to keep my brother. If you want, you can stay with me in the house, but you must move out of his bedroom. You will move out of the house when you are ready and if you want to. There will always be enough room for you in my home."

She gave me another room and I moved out. I was so happy. Mamuch did not follow me. Instead, he laughed and told me he did not care. At first I did not understand his attitude. It was only later when I was diagnosed with HIV and syphilis that I understood him. All along he knew I had nothing left to protect. It was a bombshell. That day I saw death staring into my eyes. But his sister was there for me. She kept me working and the salary I got was very helpful. I knew nothing about HIV/AIDS only that it kills. As for syphilis, it was completely foreign to me. I had heard stories about HIV/AIDS severally within our community, about who died and how painful their deaths were. Nobody ever went into details because most people were not educated about how it is transmitted, its signs and symptoms, its diagnosis and treatment and ways of prevention. All that my people said was that it was a disease brought from the Western world.

I was not sure I could survive it but here I am telling the story ten years since the bombshell. I owe my life to the guidance and counselling sessions and to the immediate HIV/AIDS treatment I underwent with the support of Kuliny. She too was a widow and had lost her husband to HIV. She knew what to do as soon as I told her. It was from Kuliny that I learnt about discordant couples where one can have HIV but does not transmit it to the partner. But she also said that discordant couples may not stay in that state for ever. That they still have to be careful because it is possible that they could infect each other.

The HIV bombshell was an eye-opener and I slowly started joining the dots. It was Mamuch's fault that I had never borne children. After knowing he was positive, he underwent vasectomy because he did not want us to have sick children. I guess he didn't care at all about me getting sick. It was during this period when I learnt that Mary too had a story with Mamuch. He had tried severally to sleep with her but she refused. She had never told me because she didn't want to hurt me.

It is my prayer that education on such matters arrives sooner to the vulnerable communities and individuals in South Sudan so as to help people living with HIV/AIDS and sexually transmitted diseases and also help in curbing the spreading of the disease.

For years, the memory of Mamuch pained my heart every single time I thought of him. I remember with clarity the sleepless nights' when I drowned myself in tears. The bitterness and the heartache that emerged from what was meant to be pure and sweet.

But all that is now gone. The only regret I carry with me today is how I constantly cursed God and blamed him for my miserable life. Was I blind? How was I even involving God in our story?

# The Brides' Price

*Lydia Minagano Kape*

That evening, Mercy got back home at about 7pm. She was exhausted and could barely feel her feet. She pulled a stool from the *rukuba*[5] and sat, as she gasped for breath. She needed to rest a bit before heading out to the neighbour's home to pick her children. She had left them with the neighbour when she went looking for their father who had been away from home for two days. She had been looking for him in all his favourite hangouts: bars, tea places, betting joints, friends' and relatives' homes.

Everyone knew that Peter, Mercy's husband, was an alcoholic. But he always came back home, even if it meant dragging himself on his knees. It was now two days and he had not returned. Mercy was worried-sick because of the alarming insecurity in Juba. Only two days back, thieves had broken into their neighbour's house and killed everybody. Mercy had not forgotten another incident that her friend Gune had narrated to her about the man who was killed on his way home late in the night, not so long ago. Whenever she remembered those stories, she said a silent prayer. She had looked everywhere she suspected and had still returned with no news of her husband at all. That evening, she said a loud prayer to drive away the heavy feeling that had taken refuge in her chest.

After Mercy got the children from the neighbour, she entered the *rukuba* to fix something for her children to eat before they slept. Once in the *rukuba*, she realized there was nothing to cook apart from the *medida* flour that her sister who lived in the IDP camp had given her from her household food rations. She lit the fire and added some dry wood on it. The whole *rukuba* filled with smoke. She kept on blowing the fire until it broke into flames and the smoke disappeared. On a tiny old saucepan she poured water for the porridge and set it on the fire to boil. Her mother

---

5    An open, grass-thatch house used as a kitchen.

had given her that saucepan when she got married to Peter. She vividly remembered the words her mother said as she gave her the saucepan: "My daughter," she had said, "the channel to a man's heart is his stomach. Do not let this saucepan spend a day without being put on fire." Mercy held her mouth to stable her trembling lips. She had to be strong. Her children were sitting next to her, looking at her. She could not let them see her cry. She had learnt to hold her tears in her small white eyes. Sadness filled her ebony face, her collar neck bones looked much outlined in the glow of the *rukuba* fire.

"Mama," she muttered to herself, "if only you knew that sometimes this saucepan does not smell fire for days, and I can't do anything about it." For a moment, guilt gripped her. She wondered whether her husband's behaviour could have been as a result of such days, but she dismissed the thought. "Well, he is not a baby. We are all in this together. It is not like I cook and eat alone." She mixed the *medida* flour and added to the boiling water.

When it was ready, she served each child one big mug. "Take all your *medida*. It will help you grow." She said to them.

"Tall like you, Ma," they responded.

"Yes," she said, smiling at each of them in turn.

"Okay now, ready, steady and go!" she said.

They each held their *medida* up to their mouths and did not breathe until the mugs were empty. They giggled and handed the mugs back to their mother.

By around 11pm, Mercy was still in the sitting room, waiting. She sat anxiously at the edge of an old, rusted metal chair and could not take her eyes off the old wooden wall clock that ticked loudly. The clock hung on the wall next to her marriage photo. It gave her a flashback of her marriage, a marriage that she succumbed to just not to be labelled the bad girl, the type that brings disgrace to the family, the type that disregards tradition and the elders' choice of the 'perfect' man to marry. Mercy had fought the marriage proposal because she wanted to at least complete secondary school, but she got no backing from her family. "Why do you want to finish school when we got you a husband? He will take care of you," one of her uncles had said. The flashback jolted her out of her seat in fury. She moved around the small sitting room straightening the already perfectly aligned chairs and smoothing the embroidered doilies that decorated them, in an attempt to forget about the past. "I am here now. This is what matters. That I am waiting for Peter and he is not here," she said to herself.

Mercy's eyes were drowsy with sleep and worry, but she was afraid that if she slept she would not hear Peter come in and then as usual he would beat her again for closing the door. She had ensured that her children were already in bed and asleep. She never wanted them to see and hear their father beating her, but somehow they always sneaked in on them whenever they fought. She felt that their violent relationship had affected the children. It was rare to find them happy and laughing amongst themselves. "If my husband doesn't come home now, I will run crazy," she said and walked to the coffeepot. "This black coffee spiced with ginger should keep me awake," she said as she fixed herself a glass of *jabana*.

At about 1:30 am, Mercy fell asleep on the chair. The tranquillity of the hour and the fatigue that she felt had overcome the power of *jabana*. It was about 2am, when she heard raucous bangs on the wooden door. The banging intensified and before she could reach to open, there was one wild bang and the door flew inside the room. Hardly had Mercy registered the darkness outside and the figure staggering into the house, when Peter hit her in the face.

"You stupid woman!" he shouted. "Who gave you permission to close the door when I am still out of the house? Don't you know this is my house? Don't you know I am the man of this house?" He mumbled insults as he dragged himself to the bed with a bottle of Seiko still in his hand. The aroma of the local brew made from fermented dates, yeast and sugar, filled the room.

However much Peter staggered and sometimes even fell, he never let go of his Seiko. He could lose a tooth but not spill any of his Seiko. He threw himself on the old bed and placed the bottle at the bedside. In less than five minutes he was snoring like he had won himself good sleep after a long day's work.

A few minutes later Mercy staggered up and tip-toed to the children's bedroom. "Your father is back my dear children. The waiting is finally over. Sleep well," she whispered. She was glad that the chaos in the house had not woken them up. She sat in the sitting room and pondered her situation. "What would my life be like if I had completed secondary school and married a different man? What would my life be if I left him?" The thought of leaving him bothered her so much and the more she wished it were possible to unthink it, the more she thought about it. She fell asleep while enveloped in thoughts of her life with, or without, Peter.

The pain of the bruises woke her up from sleep earlier than usual. She took some local herbs to help numb the pain. "My husband will need something to eat to deal with his hangover," she said as she dragged herself into the *rukuba* and lit fire to make *medida*. She poured the remaining flour into the pan. When the porridge was ready, she filled her husband's mug and placed it next to the bed where her husband slept. He was still asleep.

Mercy cleaned the house, showered her children and took some vegetables to the market. She always planted vegetables in her backyard. After she sold them, she bought half a kilo of dura flour[6] and salt. She got back from the market at about 2pm. She boiled the remaining vegetables with *kombo*[7] and made *asida*.[8] She was ready to serve her family a decent meal for the day.

It was not until about 4pm when Peter got out of the room. Mercy had already prepared his bath water. He showered, dressed

---

6        Sorghum flour. Millet flour is also referred to as dura.
7        Kombo is chloride made locally by pouring water in ash and sieving out the trash (Charcoal and sand.) It is used in cooking to soften some vegetables and legumes.
8        Maize Meal commonly known as posho Uganda or ugali in Kenya

up and sat under the Neem tree in their compound. He switched on his radio and loud music flooded the compound. Mercy served him his portion of vegetables and Asida and sat next to him as he ate. Until then, they had not talked about the previous night nor the nights he had spent away from home. "By the way," Mercy started, "Uncle Paul said you should call him once you are back home. He was so worried about you when I went to their place to ask if you were there. He even offered to help me search for you yesterday."

Peter fumed with rage. "How dare you look for me at my relatives' or even friends' homes? Hmm! How dare you!" he shouted.

"I am sorry but we were all worried," she said. Before she could explain, Peter grabbed her and started hitting and kicking her. His eyes were red and he still stunk of Seiko. She cried and yelled for help, but no one came. She begged him to stop hitting her but the more she begged the more he hit her. The children came and started crying and begging the father to stop but he did not seem to hear them. From the ground she saw her neighbour cross into the compound, then she felt her body weaken and her mind slip away.

She woke up several hours later. She tried to move but a hand held her down. "Don't turn on that side," she heard someone saying to her. Indeed as she regained consciousness she noticed she was in a hospital bed and a cannula with a drip was in her arm.

"Where are my children? Are they okay? Please tell me," she asked.

"They are well," the nurse said then quickly rushed out to call the doctor. The doctor held Mercy's hand and told her she would be well. "I am sorry. We tried our best but we were unable to save your baby. But thank God we saved your life."

Mercy was filled with wrath. Her two month's pregnancy was gone. This was her second miscarriage as a result of her husband's beating.

"Doctor," she called.

"Yes," the doctor responded.

"I do not want to become pregnant again," she said. "I do not want to die now and leave my children. They are too young to be left on their own."

"Yes."

"Please cut my tubes," she whispered.

"Hmm," the doctor responded non-committal.

"Will you do that for me?" she insisted.

"We have to consult your husband," The doctor said.

"Have you seen my husband here? This has nothing to do with him."

Three days later she was discharged from hospital. She felt a lot better. She was glad that she did not have to worry any longer about getting pregnant or having more children. Although Peter had not come to see her in the hospital, she knew her weakness. She would forgive him the moment she saw him. Her sister, Vicky, who had been taking care of her, accompanied her home. Mercy was happy to be back home with her children but the moment she entered the house, it disgusted her. She could still smell the blood that she had shed in the compound, and everywhere. Images of the neighbours who always gathered to watch them fight and try to separate them replayed in her mind like a film. She could hear their mummers which now sounded as loud as club music to her ears. The last fight had been one of the worst. He could have killed her.

Slowly, Mercy got up and walked to her bedroom.

"Come and help me," she called to her sister.

"What are you doing?" her sister asked.

"We are packing my clothes," she responded. Her sister stood and watched her pack all her belongings and those of her children. She packed everything in one big *ousofia* bag. The sisal was strong enough to carry everything, unlike most imported plastic bags.

"I am going back to my parents' home," she told her sister. "I am leaving Peter, this time for good."

"How? Why? Mercy, how?" the sister asked confused.

"Yes I am," Mercy said. "And I am sure you can answer all those questions yourself."

"No, you can't leave Peter. Listen to me, this is your home. You cannot leave. These things happen all the time. You think you are the only woman who gets hit?" she said. Mercy looked at her sister and continued packing, like a deaf person. Like she had not heard her. When she finished, she called her children who had run to the neighbour's house to tell them that Ma was back.

"Come. Put on your sandals. We are going."

"Where are we going, Ma?" they asked her.

"We are going to visit your grandparents at their house," she lied. The children were excited. They loved the story time and the cuddles their grandmother always gave them whenever they visited.

Her sister sighed in confusion as Mercy walked out of the door. She knew Peter would look for her and bring her back home that very day. This was not the first time she was being beaten. "Sunday was beaten too, but she didn't leave her husband. How many times would someone like me leave, if beating was reason enough to make women leave their marriages?" she asked. Mercy did not respond. Instead she walked faster.

When Mercy and her sister reached their parents' home, they found their mother cooking. She came out of the *rukuba* and gave her grandchildren grandmother's signature hug. She was happy to see her daughter and her children, but she was confused when she saw the huge *ousofia* bag full of clothes. She refrained from asking in front of the children.

Mercy joined her mother in the kitchen and she told her that she did not want that marriage anymore.

"I have come back to stay at home," she said to her mother. The *lofureka* the mother was using to stir sauce on the fire fell out of her hand.

"My daughter," she said. "Such a thing has never happened in our family. A well-raised girl cannot leave her marital house. What would people say about us? How would your father and I be looked at in this community? Failed parents? What do you want to happen to us? Hmm?"

"But mother! I have lost my baby again and he is to blame," she said. "And I almost died," she added with a shaky voice. Her mother paused and looked at her with concern and pity.

"I am so sorry you have had to go through that," the mother said. "But you cannot leave. He paid your entire bride price. You cannot just leave your marriage like that. The elders will have to meet and discuss the issue. They will let you know what to do."

Mercy tried to make her mother understand her situation, but no amount of words could justify her reasons for leaving. Later in the evening her father called her to tell her she must go back to her marital house.

"Such issues can be solved amicably," he said.

Mercy did not leave. The following day her uncles, who had organized her arranged marriage, held a family meeting to address the issue. In the meeting, one uncle stood up, cleared his throat and said, "There is nothing to discuss here. Since when are marriages ended because of a simple fight between a husband and a wife? That man is from a respectable family. Didn't you see them when they came to ask for Mercy's hand? Besides, Peter paid her entire bride price, so she has to go back." All the elders agreed and they called Mercy and told her that they had decided that she would return to her marital home. Just like that, her fate was dictated again.

Looking on the ground, she gathered all the courage and said to them, "I am sorry, elders, but I am not going back."

"We are not asking your opinion," the elder chairing the meeting said.

"I am sorry elders. I am sorry. I am sorry. And I pray you forgive me because I am not going back," she said. "Do you want that man to kill me then you come and wail over my body in order for you to know that there is a big problem?"

"But you have not died," an elder with missing teeth in his lower gum said. Mercy looked away in disgust and started addressing her father.

"My father, do not listen to them," she said.

"Calm down my daughter. You are our visitor. Stay until you are ready to go back to your home. Until you get well. In a week or so you will be strong enough to go back," her father said.

Mercy realized that no amount of negotiation was going to set her free. She was happy that they had allowed her to stay a few more days. She would be strong enough to be on her own and to start a new life. She thanked God for her savings which she knew would enable her pay rent and start a small business. "There's always a way," she said to herself as she walked away. "After all, it has been a struggle even in Peter's home. I will survive."

# I will come back for you

*Chol Tut Gatkek*

Nyamal was 14 years old and in primary seven when she noticed that her mother had a problem, but she did not know what it was. She lived with her parents on the outskirts of Nasir town in South Sudan. Her parents were always happy about her performance at school and encouraged her to never give up. When the term ended and her mother did not ask to look at her report, she started to worry. Her mother was always the first one to read her report card. She decided to ask her what the problem was.

"I am pregnant and I have some complications," her mother said.

"You should go to hospital then," Nyamal told her mother.

"I am not able to go to hospital because of the long distance. That is why I have not even been able to go for regular check-ups."

Nyamal was not happy. One evening, she called her parents and spoke to them.

"My parents, I have a dream," she said.

"What is your dream about?" Her father asked.

"I want to be a doctor and build a hospital. I am not happy that people travel so far to get treatment in Nasir, several kilometres away, even when they need immediate medical attention. When I become a doctor, I will build a hospital for our people. That is my dream, and God help me."

"That is wonderful my dear! I am very happy and I am sure you will do it. What you need to do now is work hard because people who want to be doctors are expected to score high marks. I will support you."

Nyamal's mother was seated supporting her back with the stick which is used for fixing mosquito nets in the evenings. She was quiet as she listened to the conversation between her daughter and her husband.

That evening her condition worsened. Her husband looked for people in the village to help carry her to the hospital in Nasir. As they prepared to start the journey, they heard sound of an airplane. It hovered in the sky until the villagers were awash with fear. Those who had come to help carry the patient were all shaking like leaves in the wind. It was a period of war and in the past, such planes had not carried any good news. People moved out of their houses and were just staring at the sky while others started running into hiding. Within a short time, the plane started dropping bombs everywhere in the village. People ran in all directions. The twilight turned dark grey and people could no longer see each other. They ran as they cried out names of their loved ones. After some minutes, ground force attackers arrived. They raided and burnt down houses. Soon the White Army,[9] which was protecting the village responded to the attack. The men who could fight joined them. Nyamal's father was among them because he wanted this to end so he could take his wife to hospital.

Nyamal joined those running for dear life but when she looked around and could not see her mother among the people, she ran back home. Her mother had crawled back into the house and was lying in her room. She sat beside her and desperately prayed for the gunfire to die down but the shooting was increasing every second. She could hear that it was coming closer. She held her mother's hands and refused to let go. "Mother! Mother! Mother!" she just kept saying.

"Nyamal, go. Go and follow those running. When this is over and you are safe, you will come back for me. Go," whispered her mother in a shaky voice.

"No mother. I can't. I can't leave you. They will kill you!"

"Go. We must not die together. Please go, my daughter, and be at peace. I will not die. Go!"

Nyamal let go of her mother's hands. She closed her eyes and walked out of the house, leaving her mother behind. "I will

---

9     The white army was a militia group of young Nuer men who worked together to defend their communities.

     *No Time to Mourn*

come back for you, mother. I will," she said, without looking back at her mother nor at their house. She ran and followed the crowd as her mother had instructed. After walking for about one hour she located her uncle's wife among the moving crowds. Bombs kept falling and shattering everything in the village. Fleeing crowds moved on. One evening turned into many days and nights of walking. Nyamal continued the journey with her aunt.

Her father did not stay with the fighters. After they were defeated and the attacking army proceeded to take control of Nasir town and surrounding villages, the locals who had joined the White Army to defend the community moved back into burning villages to salvage what they could. Later they followed the fleeing groups.

After some days he found his daughter and told her what had happened to their home. "The house in which we left your mother was burnt down," he said to her. Nyamal did not ask any questions. Her mother had been too weak to escape anything, let alone, a hungry fire. They proceeded with the journey. There was no time for them to mourn her. A few days later the father told her that he needed to go back.

"I need to go and monitor the situation in the village and look for an opportunity to bury your mother," he said. ''You are close to the Ethiopian border and I know you are now safe," he told her. Nyamal did not respond. It was as if a stone sat in her throat and she could not speak. Her father turned to his brother's wife and said, "Go with my daughter. Take good care of her. And please, I beg of you, let my daughter go to school as soon as there is opportunity. For now, I do not know when or where we shall meet next. But we shall."

"Hmm," the aunt nodded and looked away. "Let's go," she said to Nyamal and they walked away from her father. Again, Nyamal did not look back. The words she said to her mother bounced back and got stuck in her throat, *"I will come back for you... come back for you...back for you...for you...you..."*

They were registered at the reception centre across the Ethiopian border and then taken to the first refugee camp called Lietshure. Later they were transferred to Jawe refugee camp where they were registered under UNHCR and their refugee status confirmed. In the second week after their arrival, Nyamal reminded her aunt about her father's wish for her to be taken to school. The aunt took her to the camp school and she registered in primary seven. She was grateful that at least she lived with her aunt. Some people had no relative in the camp. However, the absence of her mother sat on her chest like a grinding stone.

Months passed and her father never showed up. Her aunt who had been supportive, changed and became very harsh. Life became stressful at home, as the aunt had different plans for her. Nyamal's presence in the classroom was her own struggle. She pushed on and passed her primary examinations and went to a nearby secondary school. Some people, especially her aunt's relatives, would ask to have sex with her, but she refused. Sometimes her aunt encouraged them and even tried to coerce her, but she could not agree. She insisted and told everyone who came to her, that she was not ready for such relationships.

According to her community's traditions, she was approaching the right age for marriage. Her aunt wanted her to get married so that she could enjoy the bride wealth. She connived with Nyamal's uncle, Gatluak, who lived with them. The plan was for him to attack Nyamal and beat her at any opportunity until she would decide to choose marriage over intense violence.

Days passed and examinations were approaching fast. One evening, the physics teacher decided to keep students at school longer, for coaching. Nyamal decided to attend since she felt she could do with additional support in the subject. That day she arrived home almost one hour later than the usual time. That was the trigger for Gatluak to strike. She found him inside the house with a bundle of sticks. She had just started to remove her uniform when he approached her.

"Where have you been?" he asked, ignoring her naked body.

"I was at school. I remained behind to attend a physics lesson. I am not very good at physics and so I decided to attend the class."

"Liar! Who do you think you are, to lie to me?"

She was shocked by his anger. She remained standing with her uniform halfway down her waist.

"Tonight we shall see who is more clever," he said as he jumped and hit her with a stick. Nyamal's uniform dropped onto the floor, leaving her half-naked. She ran out of the room but he grabbed her and pushed her down in the dust outside the house. "I have to deal with you today," he said. He hit her arms and face. Blood gushed out everywhere like a broken water tap. She shouted and called for help, but no one showed up. She continued shouting until she got tired and her voice became faint.

Fortunately for Nyamal, their home was next to the road through the camp. Two men who were passing by rescued her from her uncle's wrath. They asked the aunt who had just come out of the house to explain what was happening, but she just told them to leave her home. "This is a family matter which we shall sort out ourselves. This girl is stubborn. She does not respect elders," she lied.

"Stop threatening us!" they told her. "You know we can arrest you. Unless you have forgotten that we are community leaders in the camp. You two must take this girl to the clinic because as you can see, she is bleeding all over."

Not only did Gatluak refuse to take Nyamal for treatment, he also wanted to continue beating her in front of the community leaders. He became so violent that they had to call the community police to arrest him. That is when the situation calmed down and Nyamal was taken to the clinic.

The next day Gatluak was released and the matter was brought to the community leaders for discussion. He spoke first.

"I am a paternal uncle to this girl, and this is a family issue. I don't see any reason why I must explain anything to any of you. I wasn't fighting anyone else, but my niece. And I have all the right to discipline her when she goes wrong," he said.

"But she is not your daughter. And even if she was, you have no right over anyone's life. This child deserves life even if she might have wronged you," the camp leaders said.

"If you want to know, let me tell you. This woman you call a child, goes to school, but she does not return home as expected. She returns several hours after the normal time. This time I am warning her, there is no more going to school. Other girls her age are already useful and bearing children. I want her to concentrate on being a home-maker in preparation for marriage. I am part of her family and I must ensure that she does not become an embarrassment to us."

"Is that what the child wants?" the chairman asked.

"It does not matter what she wants. The family decides."

"That is not true. Maybe we would have left the family to decide if she was with her parents. But she is not. Child, what do you say?"

"I respect my uncle, but I am sorry to say that he is telling lies. I delayed at school only yesterday and for only one hour, to attend a physics remedial class. That is why he beat me. You can ask my classmates and the physics teacher. It is also because my aunt requested me to accept her nephew to be my lover and I refused."

"Nyamal! You talk too much, as if you have forgotten who is responsible for you," the aunt said.

"You should understand her," the chairman said. The community leaders asked them to stop swearing, forgive one another and go back home together peacefully. "Let the girl take her final examination without disturbance. You must not beat her up again. And if you do, we shall take action against the family and even report you to the Ethiopian authorities," they warned. Gatluak and his sister agreed to the conditions and they did not touch her again although they warned her that if she reported anything to the authorities, they would kill her. But she no longer feared them. She knew that reporting them to the Ethiopian government would end their stay and she knew that they did not want to start roaming again. The chairman had explained everything to her.

A few months later, her father came to visit them at the camp for the first time. When she heard his voice, it was like a dream. She wanted to run to him, but her legs felt like they were tied together. She just remained standing in one spot for several minutes. Even when, after some minutes, she came out and saw him standing in the compound, she did not believe it. She was so overwhelmed with emotion that she stopped in the doorway, smiling and crying at the same time.

"It's me," her father said to her. "Come over, my daughter." She walked over and sat next to him. He held her arms in front of her and looked at her. It had been several years. Nyamal was no longer the child who crossed the border with her aunt but a beautiful young woman. "How have you been?" he asked her. Instead of responding she broke into wails. She cried so loud that everybody in the house gathered around her.

"She is so happy to see you," the aunt said.

"But that should not make you cry my daughter," the father said.

"You will not leave me here father," she finally spoke.

"But I have just come. How can you start talking about me leaving you?"

"Because I have suffered in this house. See?" she said displaying the scars on her arms and legs.

"Won't you let your father rest before you display your drama?" Gatluak tried to dismiss her.

"It is okay. Leave her. What happened to you?"

"What do you think happened to her? She lives with people. She is part of this household and she gets disciplined like any other child when there is need," Gatluak jumped into the conversation. "You cannot come here and start asking about what happened to your daughter before you even greet us."

"Father, I was beaten by these people because of school. They have told me to stop going to school. They want me to get married."

"What are you talking about? If you want to go with your father you should not smear us with blood," the aunt said pulling at her ears. "You are a disgrace!" she continued. "You go to school and return in the middle of the night and you want us to say thank you! Eh? You must know that we are not raising a wild tree but a child."

"I was rescued by two men who told them never to beat me again."

"Hehehehe! Why are you telling lies? Do those men live in my house? If I wanted to beat you, I would beat you. No one would give me instructions in my home."

"I understand," her father said. "This girl is your child."

"Father," Nyamal addressed the father. "You do not believe me?"

"I believe you. I am here for you now. I will make sure that no one deprives you of your dream."

"You are not leaving me here," she said.

"It is okay my daughter," he said, looking from Gatluak to the aunt. "Now go back to your chores."

As soon as Nyamal left, he asked the aunt what had happened between them. "You are her mother," he said. "Why is she is speaking the way she is speaking?"

"It is true I beat her," the aunt said. "But I beat her like I would beat any other child, even my child," she said.

"Hmm. I understand. But, I beseech you, do not continue talking to her about marriage. She is just a child," he said.

"Let your ancestors not hear you. At what age was your wife when you married her?" Gatluak asked.

"And where is my wife now? Hmm? Where is she? When they tell you not to carry your child using dog skin and you say it's ok because you used it to carry your late child, you have a problem. You cannot refer to my wife who is not on earth anymore. But let us go and sleep. I am happy to be here," he said.

We are happy to receive you."

Nyamal's father did not sleep. The pain in his daughter's voice could not allow him sleep. Yet he did not seem to have many choices. After the death of his wife, he had decided to stay in his village and wait for normalcy, which was taking years to return. Raids were still the order of the day. Schools were still closed and no children were going to school in his village. He had to choose between taking Nyamal away and ending her education and leaving her behind with the brutal relatives so she could remain in school. When morning came, he called her and asked her to take him to the men who rescued her. She did not know their homes but luckily, she found one of them seated under the big fig tree whose knotted roots told of its age. They usually held their community meetings under its shed. The father introduced himself and appreciated the man for saving his daughter.

"It is our duty. Your daughter is not the only child being tortured in this camp. Many children are suffering," he said. "When war happens, it does not just end with the frontline. Every space we are in becomes a battlefield."

"That is true. We appreciate you elder," Nyamal's father said. "And now, I beg you, I want you to be her father. I am leaving her in your hands."

"I am sorry, my household is full. I am not able to take her on," he said.

"I mean, she will continue to stay with her aunt but I want you to help me keep an eye on her. You see, I can't take her back with me because there are no schools where I am. Yet, I know, she wants to complete school. Life is hard here, but she is able to go to school," he continued. "And I am going to warn my people. I am warning them! They should never dare touch my daughter!"

"Calm down brother," the man said.

"Not ever again," he said standing up to leave.

He stayed a few more days and used every opportunity to speak to Nyamal and assure her that all would be well.

"You will forget all the suffering once you set up your hospital," he teased her, and they laughed together.

"And you will be the chief guest at the opening ceremony," Nyamal teased him back.

When he left, she was so sad but she tried to preoccupy her mind with thoughts about the day she would open her hospital back home. Surely the universe would hear her prayer.

When the bullet was shot

# Run

*Lydia Minagano Kape*

When the bullet was shot,
They shouted run
Instead, I stood still
And watched
As gunpowder filled lonely air
I wondered; what is it that I have to run from?
Death?
Why would I run from death?
When I have died countless times already
See, this body is a tomb
A walking dead
A ghost
I have buried enough pieces of me
To form a cemetery
I die every time a bullet cuts a branch off my family tree
Don't you sometimes wonder why I buy myself flowers?
These martyrs that rest in me
I crown them,
Water their roots
Hoping they will re-live in me,
I want to be here when they breathe again.

# The Cessation of Life

*Theresa Nyalony Gatwang*

Today I am with Ruey,
And before I know it,
You have him captive.

You who does not have acquaintances,
You who is callous
Dreadful
You who hands life *jaildom*
Without trial.

You make a widow childless,
Make a child orphan,
You
Take away the only eye of a cripple.

# Money

*Veoulla Baker Ayul*

Money.
Something that never felt right in my hands.
Money.
Something that makes people crumble as quickly as sand.
Money.
Something that makes me feel guilty, it pollutes the brain and leaves it filthy.
Money.
It's no longer a metaphorical form of worth, but rather a mark left on people since birth.
Money.
Taken from trees into the blood-stained hands of environmental thieves.
Money.
It brings death and life; without it old creeps wouldn't have new wives.
Money.
It used to be fair, but we destroyed it and there is no repair.

# Ajak's Achievement Shop

*Nyankiir Nyandeng Chaat*

Dear Mr. Ajak,
*"Ana Halawa, Ana Halawa,"* I would say,
Pointing at your sweets when I came to your shop every morning.
You always laughed at my inadequate Arabic
Adding one more sweet,
One more word to my vocabulary;
*"Shukran,* Mr. Ajak," I would say and go away.

I miss chatting with my friends
At your *smokie pasua*[10] joint outside *Ajak's Achievement Shop*,
As you loved to call it.
Pride laced your words every time you spoke of it.
Your shop stood on the foundation of your blood,
Sweat and tears, traded away with the last penny scraped from your coffers.
Your vision was finally realised.
"This will secure my family,"
Your cracked-tooth-smile showed,
When you talked about the education of your strong-headed daughters.

It shakes me now
How all that was taken out of your hands,
Glass shattered,
Collapsed wall,
Bullet-holed ceiling,
Sugar in the salt,
Rice in the oil,
Broken bottles.
Blood.

---

10      Smokie pasua are sausages split and topped with tomato and chili sauce, a common street food in East Africa.

The chaos in the shop,
The chaos in the nation
All took residence inside of you,

Replacing everything else that had been there, including
Achievement Shop.
I do think about it constantly,
Little progress nipped in the bud.
I think about you too.
Live on Mr Ajak.
Let your spirit continue to pave way for your strong-headed
daughters.
They will soon be your achievement.
Who knows?
They might be the force to transform chaos to order.

# A War Child's Alphabet

*Suzan Voga Duffee*

A for army,
Belong or suffer.
B for bullets,
Obtain at all cost.
C for courage,
Genuine or feigned.
D for the dead,
We've lost all count.
E for enemy,
Hard to define.
F for fight,
A worthy cause? I wonder.
G for gun,
The bigger the better.
H for hungry,
Story of my country.
I for injured,
Physically and psychologically.
J for justice,
What we're fighting for, right?
K for killed,
Spilling the blood of women and children.
L for landmine,
A limb lost.
M for mother,
I had one.
N for naked,
Besides one short.
O for opposition,
Not any different.
P for power,

Abused by those who hold it.
Q for quarrel,
Causing nothing but havoc.
R for revenge,
Oh what a vicious cycle.
S for suffer,
Sparing no one.
T for tired,
Show me someone who is not.
U for uniform,
Equal to power.
V for vain,
How useless can we be?
W for war,
You've already made history.
X for xenophobia,
Fear anyone and everyone.
Y for yearning,
For a return to home.
Z for zealous,
If only for peace.

# Home in Mutiny

*Alith Cyer Mayar Cyerdit*

Home is in Mutiny,
Sons of the Southern Soil,
The land of the free.
Do we know where we are going?

Children of the South
Were slaughtered like sheep,
To become mausoleums and mass graves,
Stuck in mud we could not swim.

We would celebrate no martyr,
If you never took the matter to the front
Of this run
Of no return.

You took weapons,
Amidst masses of confusion.
To silence torture,
And support oppressive regimes.

You birthed Anyanya,
By forming a mighty Army,
The mighty venom,
Against the South.

Here I am,
A thirsty citizen.
Looking for answers in protocols,
But I am told, "Shut up child! It isn't your time."

Mama,
Where are you?
We want to walk with your old spirit,
To lighten this journey of South Sudan.

# Pure Cotton
*Lucy Kiden Lulu*

Cease fire,

What cease fire?
When gunshots are popping
Like fireworks in the night sky?

Does fire put out fire?
Does a stray bullet know where it belongs?

What is ceasefire?

When fear in the air
Sticks to our bodies like a wet blanket
When babies know to hold their cry,

What is ceasefire?

After rape has robbed women
Of their ribbons,
And flies?
They rise with stench of rotting flesh

What is Ceasefire?
When children keep vigil
Over dead bodies brewing oil for future drill

What is ceasefire?
When a camouflaged figure
Sends shivers to the bone
When nights are dreaded
Because darkness

Leaves behind untold tales,
Of pain and sorrow

What is ceasefire?

When insatiable blood thirst
Drinks from the innocent
When over and over
The ceasing of fire is only a myth?

What is Ceasefire
When scars imprinted
Cannot be erased
When darkness stains
Pure cotton memory

What is Ceasefire
Without fire ceasing?

# Men-struation
*Alith Cyer Mayar Cyerdit*

You don't know the history of my pain.

I am Junub
A woman in end-less men-struation
Buying daily your pads to c-over and protect my skirt from stains
I continue to bleed
afr-aid to speak of my periods

But now I say, "I am in pain, help me."

Silent guns shoot through my womb
23, 32, 10
The pad seller continues to pray for
income

I continue to men-struate
Loose so much blood
Staining.

# Here, chickens are not vegetarian

*Nyakoda Joak Mundit*

On that fateful day, 21 December 2013, I and a few other relatives reached home in Malakal, fleeing the hell that had broken out in Juba. At first, Malakal seemed peaceful. The greenness was relieving, and calm enough to settle my nostalgia for Juba. We were the most immediate neighbours to the military base in Malakal, and the area was supposed to be safe. We were not happy having to relocate from Juba in such haste, but it was okay. We were home.

But the calm did not last long. Just two days after our arrival, fighting started in Malakal. I guess we had already overstayed our welcome.

Eeh! I had never given much thought to the sounds of guns. It was in Malakal that I started paying attention to gun sounds. All guns make loud sounds, but the caterpillar is the loudest. It shakes the ground. You feel it in your feet, and feel it in your legs, and feel it in your whole body. The sound of the caterpillar fills your ears until it blocks out everything else. We could not bear it any longer. It was time to move on, but the question was, to where?

We decided to move to the compound of the peacekeepers base. It was supposedly a short journey of about one hour and thirty minutes, but it was not an easy one. In fact, it felt like we were walking for forever because my aunt who was moving with us had a full-term pregnancy. War is blind. War is deaf. War is war. We had barely covered half the journey when her water broke. The baby seemed not to know that we were in the midst of war. But so did God, I thought. How could he let any mother go into labour in such a situation? My aunt gave birth right there, at the roadside, and it was a normal delivery and a healthy baby girl. We tore our clothes off our backs and we covered the little thing. I said to myself, *I wish this child knew. It would have waited just a little longer before coming out.* We waited with my aunt for only a short while then we resumed our journey. We held the baby and my aunt walked with us.

To our dismay, when we got to the UN base, the main gates were locked. We found people who had reached before us waiting outside, and we joined them. UN gates are impenetrable. Even when you are at the gate, there might as well be continents between you and the inside. We stood outside, desperately waiting to be let in, but all in vain. People started clearing bushes to rest their tired limbs. Little did we know that this would be home for a few more days, before we could be granted entrance into the gated compound. Do not ask me how my aunt kept her baby safe from the 23rd to the 28th of December, but she did. Every morning I would look at the baby and look away. How do you look such a baby in the eye? I knew that even though her physical eyes might not see yet, her inner eyes sensed the pain surrounding her.

When the UN troops finally opened the gates, it was like we were on a merry go round because they opened a gate on the opposite side from where we were and only spoke to us through the microphone to give us instructions of how to walk around the base. The UN base is huge. We packed our blankets and saucepans again and set them on our heads. Little children and old women followed closely behind us. As we walked, I caught site of an elderly woman who could barely walk. She briefly became my walking partner as I tried to share my little energy with her. After only a short distance, she started coughing. I stood back with her as people moved on. Her chest heaved. Her body shook when she tried to speak. I stayed. Finally she managed to speak:

"*Yabinti, anamabegder.*"[11]

At first I did not understand what she meant, but her body language was clear. I could see she was too exhausted and weak to move on. That must be what she was trying to tell me. She rested her stick down and bent slowly and sat down, leaning against the UN wall. I squatted next to her and watched her as life begun to ebb out of her body. Slowly, she reached her ankle and removed her anklet made of white beads. Her shaking hand found my leg and she placed the anklet on my ankle.

11      My daughter, I can't do it.

"*Kede ita safir be al salama,*"[12] she said and slowly, very slowly, her eyes closed. That was it. She had breathed her last. I was perplexed and I wondered to myself, *would her family ever know of that moment?* I had not even talked to her to find out where she came from or who her relatives were. Anger, guilt, and confusion gnawed at my heart. I stepped away and joined the trek. I never looked behind. I still wear the anklet on the ankle where she placed it. I have never removed it.

Finally we made it to the open gate. People gushed in like water as if they had not waited for days outside the high walls! We rushed into every space available. I got into a tent and I put my luggage on the floor. I knew I had finally found a home. Even for a day or two. I took a deep breath and huddled in a corner. It did not even take a minute before I and other people who had followed me were asked to move out. We had not realised these were staff tents. We moved out and were directed to muddy bushes where we were told to clear and settle. Every single day was becoming a nightmare. I went to where I had been directed and instead sat down waiting for the night to take away the pain of the day.

The next morning, I was still lying on the ground when my aunt called me. I wondered why she was calling, and I almost pretended not to have heard her. We had barely settled and rested. And besides, what were we waking up to?

"Nyajuju," she said.

"Yes," I answered.

"Come with me. Let's go and get my bag."

"Your bag? Where is your bag Aunt Minmin?"

"It is at the World Food Programme Office. It was brought from Juba. I asked somebody to send it through World Food Program in Juba."

"Are you sure it is there?"

"Yes, I am. I am sure they did send it. And you see, that bag has some bed-sheets. In this cold and with this one," she said pointing at the baby, "the bed-sheets in there will help us."

"Hmm," I grunted.

_____
12   May your journey be smooth.

What I really wanted to tell her was that I was too tired to start another journey. But when I remembered the night cold and saw the baby in her hands, my lips clung tightly together and I did not utter any other objection. I stood up and joined her. We looked around and cast the baby in the hands of the woman next to her. In such a situation many things do not matter.

"We are coming back in a few minutes," Aunt Minmin said to the woman.

"We will see you when you return," the woman said looking at the baby and then looking away. Aunt Minmin looked away too. My stomach made a noise. I tightened my muscles to stifle it. I swallowed air and felt it move through my throat to my stomach.

"I do not know the way to World Food Programme," I retorted. "Do you know it?"

"I know the route, yes. Just follow me," she responded.

"Do you know how far it is from here?" I asked.

"I am not sure, but it could be about two-hours walking maybe," she said, and I realised that she was not thinking about the distance.

"I see," I responded.

Two hours could turn into three or four. I know how people give directions, especially if they know that the person asking has no idea of their bearings.

We started walking.

"There, that's the route we have to follow," she said pointing to a road across the UN gate. In a few minutes we were on the road. Aunt Minmin took lead. I trotted behind her like a shadow.

We walked in silence but sometimes said a word or two to each other. There were no other people on the road. We walked on and on, then we saw vultures. They were so in charge of the road that they did not fly away or even recognise our presence. Then we saw why, as we came closer. Several lifeless human bodies lay on the road. They each lay in their own position depending on when and how they had experienced their last breath. There were dogs too. Dogs that had a few days back been thin domestic animals were now fat, healthy, and wild. Perhaps they had already forgotten their masters. Perhaps their masters were among the bodies on the road. I wondered whether a dog could identify and reject to partake of the body of its master. Would a dog maintain its loyalty in such a situation?

We kept on walking. We had to get the bag and save ourselves from cold. More bodies lay ahead. They stretched and melted on the road and on pavements. More dogs ran around, feasting and playing with whatever part of the human body they wanted.

A few metres from World Food Programme we saw chickens in a cocky fight. They too had become wild. They were fighting over a long intestine stretching from a body close by. I turned and looked at Aunt Minmin.

"Chickens?" I murmured

"Hmm. Here, chickens are not vegetarian," she said.

The chickens pulled at the intestine and we waited for it to snap but it did not. I closed my eyes and held my stomach.

"Let's go," my aunt said.

"Hmm," I grunted. I had not even realised that I had stopped walking. Aunt Minmin held my arm and dragged me along. We passed more bodies, but we walked on.

By the time we reached the gate of World Food Programme, we did not even have the strength to knock. Later we tried to knock and hit at the huge doors with our hands, but there was no response. We picked stones and used them to knock but still all was silent inside. Ordinarily there would have been policemen at the gate, but there was no body.

"The bodies," Aunt Minmin said out of the blue.

"Hmm," I responded.

We stood at the gate for several minutes, but those huge metallic doors never opened. "Let's get away from here. This place can't possibly have people," Aunt said.

"And your bag? What do you think happened?" I dared ask.

"Maybe it never came. Let's go. I left the baby behind."

"Yes," I responded but my feet did not move. I was thinking about the journey back.

# It Was Taboo
*Abai Hellen Mayom*

On June 13 1984, seven girls I knew very well left our village – Gok Nyala, in Darfur, to join the liberation struggle in the bush as part of the Katiba Bannat Women's Battalion. One week after they left, I also dropped out of school, abandoned the care of my parents and family and followed them. It did not matter that I was only 16 years old. We never spoke together about our intention to join the bush, but there was a silent understanding among students that we too had an obligation to contribute to the fight for the rights and human dignity of Southern Sudanese, which were being trampled upon by the political leaders from the Arab North.

Many people wondered why we left school at such a tender age, but there are things that cannot wait. Although we were young, we already understood the importance of liberation struggle from our parents and from some of our peers who would share bits and pieces of information. There was also a community forum led by Dr. John Garang of the Sudan People's Liberation Army (SPLA), where adults would discuss the "new wave of liberation." They even talked about the struggle of the Anyanya II before Garang. In addition, from the dilapidated state of schools, hospitals and general poverty, we knew something was not right. SPLA revolutionaries would sneak into schools and communities and preach about better education and greener pastures for a liberated *Southern Sudan*.

The day I left home, I never informed my parents. I knew they would never allow me to go to the bush. As much as our parents wanted independence, they did not think that it was for their children to fight for. And maybe they were right. Experiences of the bush are totally unpredictable. Some make it while others do not.

It was around noon when I cast my small backpack over my shoulder and walked away from home. I passed one home after the other, hoping and praying that no one would ask me where I was heading. I had already prepared answers in my head. I left alone because in those days, it was taboo to talk about joining the armed struggle. You could not know when it was safe to speak about it because there were informers who sometimes betrayed unsuspecting patriots. After I walked for several hours, I met a group of other young people who were also joining the movement. I could identify them because they were already under the stewardship of the SPLA Jamus (meaning buffalo) Battalion, whose mobilisation taskforce had an ongoing recruitment. After moving for several kilometres, we entered a bush that stretched into a forest.

Deep into the forest in Eastern Rumbek, we were confronted by the Adutich River and had to cross. There was no other way to join the team on the other side. The river was very terrifying, but we all felt it would be even more terrifying to go back home and sit with our families under the rule of terror. That's why we were all joining the movement voluntarily in the first place. One by one, people crossed to the other side. When it was my turn, I was unsuccessful and fell into the running water. I struggled, but fortunately, it was not so deep a river. I managed to cross.

Shortly after crossing the river, we found guerrillas who had come to receive us. I found the other seven girls who had left my village also with the guerrillas. We were very excited to find each other. We embraced and exchanged pleasantries. They asked me how their families were. They were happy that I was joining the movement too. Our leaders welcomed us, registered us, and gave us a briefing. We were officially freedom fighters. They asked us about our future plans and we felt relief as they convinced us that it was a just cause and that we were in safe hands. They said that we would all reap the fruits of the liberation once war was over. They told us not to worry about missing school as they would later enrol us into schools. At the end of the registration process, it felt like the war was going to be over in just a few months or even days.

The following morning, we were told we were heading to Ethiopia, and we began our journey. We did not have any form of transport. Our only option was to walk till we reached our destination. We moved on bare feet day and night, for very many miles. We could not even count the distance we were covering because we were walking through the bushes. During the discreet mobilization in villages, the soldiers were given cows, goats, and flour. Sometimes the food would be scarce, I must say, but fortunately we didn't starve. Some local leaders even gave in their children as contributions to the movement. That was sobering.

The bushes were infested with mosquitoes which bit us even during the day. We were hit by rain and when it was not raining, the sun was extremely hot. But we walked on. On many occasions, we had no water for bathing because some of the areas we went through were like deserts. My age-mates and I, especially the seven girls from my village, missed our families so much. It was dreadful in the first months of being away from home. Many times we regretted leaving our homes but truth be told, we could not go back. We actually had no way of going back. We had to endure the situation and constantly prayed to God for strength and protection.

As we got closer to Ethiopia, we encountered an ambush by the Sudanese army. I believe it was only God who saved us from being hit because the bullets came like rain! We were shot at from all directions, but somehow we survived until our colleagues were able to repel the government forces. And I must say it was chaotic, as we the new recruits were running back and forth while bullets were flying. I remember my mind stopped thinking at that time and I just started crying and shouting. War can make you lose your head. My mind literary stood still. I could not think. I could not imagine anything. Everything was so terrifying.

During that ambush, one of the volunteers who was carrying a baby belonging to our commander, Ajuong Makwer, wanted to abandon the baby and leave it to die in the wild, I guess because the baby was an inconvenience and a burden to him.

Ajuong Makwer was at the frontline commanding the soldiers managing the ambush. We, especially the girls, were shocked at the cruelty of war. How could anyone think of abandoning a live baby to save himself? It was so strange. At the same time, I could not imagine what I would have done had I been the one carrying the baby. I was afraid to think of being in his shoes.

When I think about it now, I wonder whether the volunteer was actually trying to save the child by hiding him in the bush. Fortunately, the volunteer decided to proceed with the baby.

At the end of the ambush there were heavy casualties. One of the most prominent commanders at the time, Deng Alor Kuol, got shot on his thigh. After the gun-shots had stopped, we continued with our journey. The ambush came about two days before we reached the Ethiopian border.

The journey from our homes to Ethiopia took us three solid months. As soon as we crossed, we went to a refugee camp called Itang. We spent a few weeks in Itang while preparing to go to the army training centre called Bilpam, which was about three hours away. Itang was a civilian refugee camp, whereas Bilpam was an SPLA military base. At Bilpam, I met my maternal uncle, Maker Joseph, who had joined the liberation struggle earlier. He was my closest relative in the bush.

***

The reality and pain of liberation struggle is something we freedom fighters and other South Sudanese hold dear. We were like a pregnant mother. However much she suffers pain of pregnancy, she still glows, and genuinely so. During the war, we enjoyed a lot of camaraderie and togetherness. I recall that at some points, I would have over twenty people in my house and, regardless of some quarrels and fights, we all managed to remain a family unit; one big struggling, but happy, family. Many households in the military bases and liberated areas shared the same spirit and accommodated even more than twenty people. Regardless of the tribulations they encountered, all shared a certain joy which kept them together till that day when independence finally came.

The night before Independence Day, we did not sleep. We were gripped with feelings of anxiety but also contentment on seeing the returns on the investment we had made on behalf of our country. People had made all sorts of sacrifices; thousands had lost their lives. Our country stood still while others progressed. The losses, pains and tears of the liberation struggle were being erased by the birth of our new nation. A sense of fulfilment and achievement filled the air. My husband and I could not stop celebrating.

I was so happy that my family members and I, especially my husband, were still alive, to witness the ceremonies and the transition. We, like many other South Sudanese had participated, contributed and sacrificed for the liberation struggle and we had suffered a lot in the process. For a long time, therefore, we looked forward to the coming of Independence Day for South Sudan. We believed that Independence would mark the end to our suffering.

I remember that when I saw the president raise the flag as a sign of South Sudan's Independence, I was filled with euphoria; a state of feeling that covered every South Sudanese at the time. I watched my husband with contentment. He was among the high profile people during the celebration. He oversaw security within Juba, the capital city of South Sudan.

The day after Independence, I walked around Juba in utter amazement at the miracle of a new nation on earth, a nation called South Sudan. My spirits were indescribable. I was almost in tears of joy. Something profoundly significant had happened to us. South Sudan had attained independence, our freedom; something that Hong Kong and many other citizens of the globe are still fighting for. It was a similar joy to that of holding a new-born, especially for parents who have tried for years to have a child. I was smiling. I was emotional. I was happy.

We spent the days that followed moving to different towns of South Sudan with the most intense joy. We talked, we laughed and we celebrated. People of South Sudan had suffered a lot during two major long wars of 1955 to 1972 and that of 1983 to 2005. The two wars will remain in the minds of the South Sudanese people and the world. J. K. Lupai 2014[13], states that, "Four million people were displaced and driven from their homes notwithstanding the high level of destruction of property and institutionalized underdevelopment as a policy to keep Southern Sudan perpetually dependent. Half a million people remained refugees in neighbouring countries. Many others got permanent disabilities and others got mad."

Jacob J. Akol[14] observes in his book, that during the war, there were savage attacks on villages in Northern Bahr el Ghazal and the upper Nile. Crops were destroyed, cattle and young children and women were killed or looted. Col. Dr Garang argued during some of his political rallies, that thousands of black Sudanese were forced into slavery in the old Sudan under the Islamic regime. It is believed that many tribes including the Bongo, Kresh, and Makaraka tribes, were virtually wiped out.

***

You must be wondering how I returned from the bush and celebrated independence and am now talking about a husband when I left home at sweet sixteen. Well, I met Kuol Deng Abot on that day when I fell into the Adutich River in Eastern Rumbek. This man who later became my husband was part of the taskforce, carrying out recruitment and registering people joining the Jamus battalion. That was our first interaction. Interestingly I do not remember anything special between us on that first day. But I remember that I was fascinated by his promise that they, the rebels,

13    Jacob K Lupai (2014), South Sudan: Issues in perspective, AISA Ltd, Kampala, Uganda
14    Jacob J. Akol, I will go the distance: A story of a 'lost' Sudanese boy of the sixties, 2005, Paulines Publications Africa, Nairobi.

would take us back to school after the struggle. We became friends as we continued to interact at the training camp.

I did my military training at Bilpam in Ethiopia. I sometimes saw comrade Kuol because he was one of the officers who would bring recruits for training to Bilpam military camp. The training took eight months. My husband and I wedded at the training centre in 1985.

Things went really fast, as they say. There was friction during the marriage proceedings due to formalities that needed to be fulfilled. There was a bit of resistance from some family members on my side, but the decision by the two of us prevailed.

I was just about to turn 17 years while he was 24years. We were both young and lacked knowledge on many family issues especially raising children. I was happy to get married. Although there were two weddings at that time, I was the first to get married among the group I had entered the bush with.

Our wedding was very interesting because my husband was not physically present. He was away on duty in another military camp at the border with Ethiopia. He was represented by his brother at the wedding and the brother later delivered me to him. In the military, it is normal to sacrifice anything in the name of duty.

There were a number of senior women like Mama Nyandeng Kerbino - the wife of Cdr. Kerobino Kuanyin Bol, Mama Rebecca Nyandeng De Mabior, and a few others who joined the bush when they were already married. These women were very inspiring to us the young ones. We watched them as they managed their roles very well, both as mothers, as wives and as soldiers. They also had time to mentor us.

Two months later, my husband left Bilpam for a cadet training programme. I had just conceived our first pregnancy. He appeared eight days to the birth of our first born. You can imagine how happy I was to see him. The good thing is that military training teaches a lot of endurance and resilience. After the birth of our baby on 6 October 1985, my husband left again for a senior cadet academy in Cuba, where he spent over nine months. I played both roles of being a mother and a father. I trained my children and disciplined them.

After the cadet training, he returned to Bilpam. We soon had our second, and then our third child. After a while, we relocated to Pochala which is towards the border of South Sudan. I will never forget how, on that journey, I carried my third born in a basin on my head. That was in 1991, after the fall of the Derg government under the leadership of Haile Mariam Mengistu. We were displaced by the incoming government and we had to run away immediately. We walked for fourteen days. Eventually we crossed the border and entered the interior of Southern Sudan. I would put the basin down to breastfeed, and then put it back on my head. When I tell my younger children this story, they just look at me, astonished, as if it is all fiction. It was a rainy season, but we moved. During warfare, you cannot decide when to move. All movements have a purpose and must be made when they must. That journey was terrible. We were hit by rain almost every day. We did not have umbrellas or raincoats.

Unfortunately, we encountered another ambush while we were on this journey. Many soldiers died in Gilo River when gunfire opened above us as we crossed.

I pay special tribute to our female colleague, a very noble soldier called Anip. She too died in Gilo. I knew Anip. We had been together in school. She was a popular girl, intelligent, talented and a liberator at heart. I recall that she once got arrested by the old Sudan security agents for speaking against oppression. Anip was in high school while I was in junior school. She was very stall and slender; one who could be described as an African beauty. At school Anip Marial Dhut would stand up for anyone she felt was marginalised. She was very active and played basketball for the school team. She was a storyteller too. As we journeyed from our village to the bush, she amused us with hilarious stories that even the taskforce soldiers would whole-heartedly join in to listen. We were all saddened by her death. Rest in peace Anip.

During the liberation war, I invariably encountered a number of challenges, but so did all of us freedom fighters. We fell sick all the time because of poor conditions in the bush. We did not have proper, or even enough, food to eat most times. Sometimes rains would not spare us, and it would be very cold. You can be at home in the evening and when a few mosquitoes attack, you think they are too many. When you are in the bush, you are in the bush. Mosquitoes are like grass and you have nowhere to run to. They bite you every single day until they get tired. At first you cannot even sleep and you fall sick, but with time you get used to it. Maybe the body immunises itself.

On other occasions we would carry heavy luggage for long distances, sometimes on empty stomachs, especially when we were relocating from one place to another, like that time when we relocated from Bilpam. Sometimes we would walk the long journeys with our children and all our property. We were lucky that the Jamus Battalion was professional. The soldiers trained us on how to survive the harsh conditions during armed struggle in the bush. They gave us both psychological and social support.

Though there are many challenges we still have to overcome as a nation, they are not comparable to the challenges we suffered under the dominant northern Arabs' rule. We, as South Sudanese, shall always remember the day we received our independence. I know for sure, that whatever happens, I will certainly continue to celebrate the 9th of July, until I enter the silence of death.

Country is Running

# Birth water

*Bigoa Chuol*

To the children whose birth water is broken by whizzing of
shrapnel
This is our portion

We know war in sunken eyes
We know it in the jabbing hunger pains
We know it in our callused, blistered feet

Home is living between two tectonic plates
Home is suspicion
Home is crouched face down on cement pavement

Deep orange skies that invite birds that squat, scrap and scavenge
Blood has made it to the ground water

We know the reeking smell of almost, entirely well
We cannot hold it to our cracked lips
So, we bite down on our children and our kin bleed

There is time to perish
But there is no time to mourn
There is time to rot
But there is no time to bury

The dead now, do not motivate our fathers to get up from under
the trees
They pour another cup
This is bottomless tea

The dead do not motivate our mothers to teach their sons substance
Our black skin hangs loose, lather with oil to keep it from running

What is sanctum on unceded land?
We say we have survived
But a new chaos embraces us softly, quietly

Fear cannot raise, it smothers
Fear cannot give nutrient to the soul

Fear punches holes in the future
Fear cannot mend them
It siphons the chaos for later

Home always comes late, if at all
Later always comes so soon

We cannot continue to swing across oceans with these mangled roots
When war breaks, we run
We do not carry our language
When war rages behind clenched teeth

To fathers that sleep with guns in their hands
But will never hold their children

Legacy does not fill the gaps
You've turned our names into weights that crush our backs
You've turned our names into sinking sand

What is legacy to torn limbs?
What is plumbing to broken spirits?
What are roots if they choke you?

We say home is so far
The same oceans sit between folks looking into each other's eyes
Our portion is silence

They imagine home is settled soot
They imagine country is running
We now know refuge is both.

# The Unending Journey

*Charity Naume Naigupai*

One evening in 1989, my father came home with a funny looking ball. It was orange in colour, oval shaped and had five black stripes running across it. I had never seen such a ball before in our beautiful village of Naagori in Yambio. It looked like the orange sun disappearing at the horizon. My immediate sister Ngbarago and I ran toward him, shouting at the top of our voices, *"Baba jja leele. Baba jja, leele!"*[15] We welcomed him back. We both jumped at him and reached out to grab the ball from his hands.

"Wait!" he shouted at us and did not release the ball.

Something was strange. My father's reaction confusing. He did not pick me or my sister and throw us up as he usually did. Instead, he hurried past us asking.

"Where is your mother?" he asked as he entered the house.

"Mama is that side," my sister responded, pointing to the side of the kitchen.

It was clear to us that whatever was bothering him was urgent and it required an immediate response or action. He scampered away into the house.

It was already late in the evening and starting to get dark. We followed our father into the house and tried to listen as he spoke to mother. We could not hear much because he spoke in undertones. His face wore a look of urgency. Young, innocent and unexposed, I wasted no time trying to listen to their whispers. I simply ran back outside to play with my *bakinde sende*,[16] cooking in empty tomato paste tins. We used the fine soil besides the grass thatched kitchen. I was playing the role of mother.

Mama came out of the house a few minutes later. The sun in the sky was oval like the ball Baba had just returned with. It was setting, reddish orange and dull, as though a heavy downpour

---

15     Yay, Baba has come!
16     Mixture of soil and water which children play with pretending it is maize or cassava meal.

was about to come. Mama spoke with women across the fence. They said the evening was angry; the clouds of fear and tension were foreshadowing the impending gloom that was about to befall the land. To us however, it was a lovely evening that allowed us to play without getting tired as we did in the hot sun. We continued to play in the twilight.

Slowly, darkness was embracing the village. My sister and I were forced to go inside the house. When Mama saw us, she screamed.

"Where is Ga Mboripai?" she asked.

"But you know she went with Aunt Joyce," I said to her.

"You mean she is not back yet?" Visiting a neighbour or a relative in the village nearby was not strange; we always did this. But mother was acting like it had suddenly become taboo.

Ga Mboripai was our youngest sister. She was about two years old. Aunt Joyce had passed by home when we were playing and she took her to visit the family. Mother was upset that my aunt had not returned the child home yet. It was getting late. She urged father to hurry and fetch the child. She told us that we had to leave.

"Where are we going Mama?" we asked her.

"Do not ask silly questions. Everybody and every family is preparing to leave town," she responded. She said that people, including my aunt's family, were all leaving town and would head into different directions. "Go fetch our child," she said turning to my father. "Aunt Joyce might leave with her to a place we do not know. Please, go!" She emphasised. "They might even forget her and leave without her." That put sense into my father's head. He jumped onto his recently bought black bicycle and rode off as fast as he could.

Mama gathered a few things randomly. She picked some basic foodstuffs from the store: cassava flour, groundnuts, cooking oil, salt, sugar, two saucepans, a few plates, cups and spoons. She entered our bedroom and picked a few clothes and shoes. She went into their bedroom and picked a few of her and Baba's clothes, some beddings, and a mattress. She dashed back and picked a flashlight.

"I had forgotten this," she said, and she stuffed the flashlight into a small cloth bag where she was putting a few other things. I followed her everywhere she went and continued asking her questions.

"Mama, why are you packing?" She ignored me. "Are we going to move to another house again?"

Our family usually moved to different houses from time to time. For a moment, I thought we were just moving to another home. My father was a pastor and sometimes would move from parish to parish.

"We are not moving to another house," she said. We are going for only a few days to a town nearby called Nzara and then we will come back."

"Why are we going to Nzara?" I asked again.

"Because the government has announced over the megaphones that people should leave Naagori," she said.

I continued asking her many other questions but she did not give much information. I began to sense that something serious was about to happen.

When my father arrived some minutes later with my sister, Mama said we were ready to leave. Baba said that we should only carry the very basics. Like Mama, he said that there was no need to take a lot of our stuff because we were only going to Nzara and after a week or two, we would be back.

Mama put the items she had sorted into two large pieces of *kitenge* cloth and tied them up into bundles. She put one bundle on my head, and she carried the other. She tied my baby sister on her back and held my other sister's hand. Baba tied a mattress and a few other things on to his bicycle. We left our three-roomed house at the roadside just like that. Everything was happening too fast.

As we approached the main road to Nzara, I saw that it was jammed with people. Many families were leaving their homes.

Moving cars and motorbikes were rushing at a very high speed. Pedestrians were being pressed against the roadside bushes, along with the people on bicycles. Some people pulled unwilling goats behind them. Sheep and dogs followed along too. Women balanced their luggage on their heads, with babies, crying on their backs. Some people were rushing in the opposite direction to go and gather their families. The two-lane dirt road was filled with dust being raised by people's feet, the cars and bicycles. The air was filled with sounds of hooting cars, honking trucks, ringing bicycle bells, motorbikes beeping, people talking on top of each other's voices, as well as the panicked cries of children.

That is how we left our beloved Naagori. Nzara never became our destination. Little did my parents know that it would be at least ten years before we returned to Naagori. This was just the beginning of our unending journey.

It was a long and tedious trek. When we reached Nzara, we met my aunt's family. They too were stranded at Nzara. Fortunately, the Bishop of the Episcopal Church of Sudan gave us a lift in a little pickup truck which belonged to the church. We were so happy because it had become clear that the rebels were advancing towards Nzara. We all squeezed onto the pickup truck – about four families. Since my father had a new bicycle, he decided to follow us slowly on his bicycle so that we meet at the border. Interestingly, when we were parting ways at Nzara, he and my mother forgot to discuss which country we would be entering. On reaching the border, the Bishop's family, whose pickup truck we were on, decided to go to the Central African Republic (CAR). Mama did not know what to do but she just prayed and hoped that Baba would not decide to enter Congo. By God's divine intervention, when Baba reached the border, he asked some people whether they had seen the Bishop's convoy and the route it could have taken. Since there was only one bishop, it was pretty easy to locate us. They directed him to the CAR side.

After my father found us, he stared moving around the village trying to locate a space to hide the two vehicles we had. We were now about 10 families. Word was going round that the rebels were after the displaced in order to get cars and of course other things to confiscate. Before night fall, my father who was most active with a heart to serve and a responsible attitude, had to act quickly with the help of a few other men, to find where to hide the cars. He had to be helpful not only because the Bishop had assisted his family, but he was his boss too. Baba was a priest back home. He became the superhero to save the day because he found a safe spot deep in the bushes where they hid the vehicles. Together with two youths, they drove the two pickups across the check point without any luggage to avoid raising suspicion. On their way out of the bush, they raised the grass so that the car trucks could not be traced – hard work. All the luggage had to be carried by head and bicycles all night to where the cars had been hidden. Thank God the plan worked. Early the following morning, we were on our way to the CAR. That's how we crossed the border and our status changed to that of refugees. We never saw that border check-point again until about ten years later.

In the little village of Bambutti where we settled, there were rumours that government soldiers were running away from the rebels and hiding in the same bushes where we were hiding. In fact, as my father took us deep into the bush one day, to identify spaces where we could hide at night, we met with one helpless *mundukuru*,[17] also trying to hide. He had no possessions whatsoever. We were all facing the same fate now.

The markets in Bambutti were closed and there was no food anywhere. Good enough for us, my parents had carried some foodstuffs. Unfortunately, one bag of cassava had oil in it which had spilled from a jerrycan of petrol which was in the vehicle that had brought us. Because there was nothing else to eat, we had to make do with the petrol-reeking *bakinde*. That was not a good idea at all because at first all of us became sick. We were all throwing up except our young cousin. Thank God we became well soon enough.

17      An Arab from Northern Sudan

After some days in the open field, my father located a church in the small town of Mboki. He asked the pastor if we could be given a space to stay. Remember my father was a pastor too. The pastor and his family were very kind. They gave us their back-veranda. Finally we were in a home, sheltered on the veranda from the sun and the rain.

One of the most painful experiences I have known as a refugee is hunger and thirst. Soon, the food we had carried got finished and there was just never enough food or water for all the people who crowded into the town from different parts of Southern Sudan. As refugees, we were only allowed to touch, eat and drink what we were given. There were many fruit trees growing in the church compound, but we were not allowed to pick or eat even the fruits that fell from the fruit trees by themselves. The trees would be filled with fruits, ripe and ready, but we were never to touch. It was only the fruit they called *citron*,[18] that was less monitored and so we would pick especially the partially rotten ones and eat them. The rest we did not touch. We were prohibited from touching even the wild fruit trees in the village. If we tried to pick any and eat them, the local people would ask us whether our grandfathers had planted those fruit trees. They would even tell us that we should go back to our country. One time when they told us this, we went back home to the veranda and told our parents that we should go back home. Our father told us that we would go back some day.

"Why not now?" I asked him.

"Because we can't," he said. "Where do you go in a country torn with conflict?"

I looked at him, and he looked at me. I did not know what to say to him. At that time, there were many things I did not quite understand, and he did not try to explain much to me. When we got fruits and food and we played, I did not think so much about Naagori, but when we had nothing to eat, I missed Naagori and wished I could just walk back, even if it meant going on my own.

---

18      Citron is a French word for a fruit in the family of lemons

We stayed for months and then years in Mboki. We even started going to school. The shade of another mango tree as big as the one where we first lived, was the Primary One classroom in the refugee school. One day I decided I would not be put down by any circumstances. That day I had walked into class (under the mango tree) late as I did most times because our home was about five kilometres from the school premises. I was bare-footed because I owned no shoes but even if I had them, I would not wear them. My feet, like most other children, were infested with jiggers. Maybe it was because of the dust at home and the dust in school under the tree. Many children in the camp had jiggers.

I shivered in the early morning biting cold of the dry season. I was dressed in a faded oversized woollen boxer as a skirt, which was held to my waist with a banana fibre. This was the only piece of cloth that fell to me when the *aliwara*[19] were being distributed to refugees in the camp. Each family could only receive one or two items per person, of the second or even third and fourth-hand clothes. Since we were many in the family, the boxer was all I could get. After reaching my class, late and hungry, I found that the teacher had given a math exercise. He spanked me and warned me against my habitual late-coming and told me to join others and do the exercise.

The pupil I sat with was busy writing his exercise. I started to write my answers. It was a difficult exercise but I knew the answers. When I finished, I leaned over to see what my neighbour was writing in his book. He was a smart child, or so I thought. He wore better clothes and was rarely in trouble. I saw that all his answers were 110. The first a question was 10-9 and my answer was 1. As soon as I saw his answers, I rubbed off all my answers and I wrote his answer in all the spaces as he had done. I did not question his answers or even think about them since he was rarely beaten by teachers. I knew he must be right.

---

19      Clothes that were distributed in the refugee camp were called aliwara by camp dwellers.

When the teacher came around to look at the answers in our books, he gave me zero over ten and he spanked me again. He spanked my neighbour too and all other children who had failed. When he went over the exercise, I realised I had got all the numbers correct in the first place before I copied from my neighbour. From then on, I decided I was smart despite my clothes. My shoe-less feet did not define what was in my head.

My new-found perspective on life helped me to excel and progress in school, and in life generally. Even when we relocated and got challenges in our family, I did not let that get in my way. I kept my head above my shoulders, which probably is the reason I am at peace with myself and with the world around me.

And guess what! I grew up. I acquired a good education with a degree, and I became an independent woman of conviction. I got married too and now I am a mother of two lovely children: Isabella and Abigail.

***

Years later, Southern Sudan becomes a country: We return home. South Sudan Roads are tarmacked. Public transport is booming. We are happy to be back home.

My husband and I board the long 60-seater bus from South Sudan heading to Kampala. We have some errands to run in Kampala. The bus slows down as it rounds off the last corner of the winding Nimule hill. In a distance, I see the roadblock. The road is under repair, forming loose gravel that clatters around the bus tires. The bus slows to a stop. A tall soldier, dressed in dark green khaki, approaches the bus entrance and orders us to come out. Passengers in front of me start to disembark onto the loose gravel outside. My husband and I follow suit. We are welcomed with the simmering midmorning heat and annoying flies knocking against each other and against our faces.

The soldier steps forward and yells at me, *"Ya wewe intah! Wen aurag?"*[20]

I am startled and I do not respond immediately. My husband, a tall and dark gentleman, steps forward and shakes his head in response to the soldier.

"No. We are not *wewes*. We are Junubians. We have the documents." He hands the soldier our two South Sudanese passports. The soldier frantically grabs the passports from his hand and stares at them. He looks confused. Then he asks sheepishly, *"Inta ma hiya?*[21]*"*

*"Ai,*[22] I am with her," my husband answers smiling, his eyes shifting between me and the soldier. I can tell it is not a smile but a show of teeth. The soldier does not seem content. He looks perplexed. He looks at my husband from head to toe as if measuring his height and then looks back at me. He asks again, *"Hiya junubi?"*[23]

I want to laugh but I do not. I am tired of these games. My husband turns and looks at me.

*"Ai.* We are together," we respond simultaneously and our lips twist into miniature smiles.

The soldier smiles back sheepishly and says, *"Yazol,"*[24] as he hands us back our passports.

"You better believe, my boss," my husband says as he receives them. They exchange a few stiff pleasantries as we proceed to the immigration.

I know it is about my light complexion and short stature. We are getting used to this kind of interaction resulting from tribal stereotypes.

---

20    Hey, you East Africans? Where are your papers? Wewe is a Kiswahili word meaning you. It is used especially among common people like market vendors and bus touts as a nickname for East African foreigners in South Sudan.
21    Are you with her?
22    Simple way of saying, yes.
23    Is she a Southerner?
24    Hey! Pronounced with a tinge of disbelief.

The orange sun disappearing at the horizon and the mean army man, remind me of Papa's orange ball that we never got to play with. Probably he left it in our house in Naagori.

As we get back on the bus, I pray and hope for a tomorrow with no prejudices.

# Echoes and Cobwebs

*Mary Kadi*

The gushing rain on the roof was soothing yet terrifying. We had not seen rain for months, yet this was supposed to be a rainy season. The sun which Mama said was hot, like the inside of the iron-sheet oven, had stubbornly refused to give way to the rain. I heard a woman tell my mother that God, high up in the sky, had stopped the rain from coming down because he was angry with the war blood which had soaked into the ground. My young mind did not comprehend what blood in the ground had to do with rain in the clouds. Nevertheless, I was relieved that it rained and I could sneak out to go and play outside for a little while before my parents came out. They were having an afternoon nap.

I was back and shivering as my teeth chattered. Why were they taking so long? I wondered. I wanted my jacket from their room as I had begun to get chills. So, I got up and walked towards their door so they could hear my footsteps and know that I needed them. As I approached the doorway, I heard them talking.

"You must understand that we have nothing else to do. Things are getting worse. We need to leave," Papa was saying. I could hear his voice cracking.

"I know Keji needs a good school. I know. You always talk about that," Mama added.

"School? You are joking. If it was just school, then we would stay."

"But maybe things will get better?"

"This is the time to move. We cannot take chances. She will survive," Papa answered.

The mention of my name worried me. I peered through the doorway and saw Mama pace up and down the room as she sometimes did when Papa would be late getting home. She kept shifting her eyes from the floor to the ceiling and back. After a while, Papa too stood up from the bed and headed for the door.

I scurried away back into the living room as fast as my little legs could carry me. I did not want to be discovered and caned for eavesdropping on a conversation I was not supposed to hear. From experience, I knew what would have happened if I had stayed. Several minutes later, Papa walked into the living room and found me crouched against the floor eyes glued on the TV screen.

"Keji why didn't you sleep? Switch off the television and go and sleep. You will not grow tall if you do not sleep during the day," he said wagging a finger at me. In my mind, I wondered how exactly I would grow tall by sleeping and added it to the long list of things I was told to do if I wanted to grow tall: eat *Lobutereng*,[25] run and not walk when I'm sent to the shop, respond when my elders call me, avoid looking big people in the eye... It was a long and confusing list.

Without a complaint, I got up and went to the bedroom we all shared. As I had predicted, as soon as I disappeared into the room, he switched the channel. I could hear the fans roaring – a roar would stop midway then continue on, sounding like a wail accompanied by a whine, like the one I made when mama pinched me for not doing my chores. I heard the commentator's voice too crackling like an old boom box. You see, our television lived on the mercy of the antenna outside. On rainy days like this, it was a puzzle of scenes that froze and framed themselves before resuming a flowing scene and then freezing again. Despite all this, it was a luxury to even have one, as many in our neighbourhood never had any. I was eternally grateful.

As I reached for my mattress, I remembered what I had overheard Papa and Mama talk about. Mama looked at me as I quietly spread the thin, worn-out mattress on the floor.

"Little-one," she called out to me as she tapped the side of the double bed that she shared with Papa. "Come on. You are lost in your thoughts again. What is the matter?" she asked.

---

25    A bitter vegetable claimed to be a natural medicine and vitamin booster

"Nothing is the matter Mama." I said. Mama always called me Little-one for as long as I could remember. "I'm just hungry and I do not really feel like sleeping," I lied. I had once heard Mama and Papa arguing about something that didn't make sense to me, but when I walked in and asked them to explain, I was instead disciplined with Mama's long stick, for interrupting and listening in to adult talk. She always kept the stick behind her bedroom door and could grab it at ease to discipline me at will. So I did not want her to know that I had been eavesdropping.

Instead of lying on the mattress, I just sat and stared at the ceiling like Mama. Mama tilted her head to one side and smiled at me.

"Keji, you do not seem happy. Is there something bothering you?" she asked.

"No Mama, nothing." I lied again.

As she pursed her lips unsure of what to say next, she pulled out a carton of flavoured milkshakes from under the bed. My eyes widened as she handed me my favourite flavour, strawberry.

"Thank you, Mama," I said smiling sheepishly at her. We both knew that Papa would not have approved of the afternoon milkshake if he were in the room, but he wasn't and this would be our little secret, like many other secrets we shared.

Several weeks passed and we had not moved. But day by day, I saw Mama piling clothes on the bed. Sometimes she called neighbours and gave away bags of clothes. Even some of my toys fell victim. When Mama asked me to select my favourite toys and put aside what I did not want any more, I thought, what an impossible task! Of course, I wanted all my toys!

With time the house became less and less cluttered. Everything was finding its space in boxes. All types of boxes lay around the house. The day had come when everything would be gone and the state of our house became echoes of silence, emptiness and cobwebs

***

We were welcomed by the simmering heat and the scorching sun of Kenya. It was Christmas day 1993. Papa's brother came to pick us up from the airport. As we drove into the city, old, yellowing billboards flew by. A wave of people seemed busy walking to and from nowhere in particular. The buildings zooming past five times the height of those I left back home. Towering so much so I had to crane my neck to see their tops. Despite it being Christmas, I had no new clothes and no new shoes to celebrate the day as was the tradition back home. I hated it, and I wished I had never come.

"You will make new friends and have new experiences," Mama told me, but I did not believe her, because she could not look me in the eye as she said those words. She held my hands and spat into them - a traditional goodbye. As she handed me over to Papa's elder brother, she told me that I would be in good hands. She still looked, teary eyed, as she spoke.

"He is your father now and you will listen to him and do what he says. You understand?" I nodded, although I did not understand a single thing.

I saw Mama's eyes open and close in quick succession, and I knew that like me, she too was struggling to contain her emotions. After spending a silent dinner with me – they were taken to the airport that night. They were gone.

Fear engulfed me.

They were moving on.

I was left behind.

I was confused and unsure of what to expect. I immediately felt that it would be years before I saw them again. From what I was told, they were leaving for Uganda. Years later, their memory would be a lingering scent of a good perfume on a windy day.

When they left, Mama left me with her gold stud earrings which I cherished and vowed to keep until we met again.

I cried so much that night, my eyes swelled with pain. For months, I had no appetite and with time I grew thin. I thought about Mama all the time: in bed, in class, in the toilet. Even while eating. It was the first time I was being left on my own without Mama. My confusion turned to anger. I constantly wondered why she had left me.

On the fateful day of their departure, I had heard Papa say to my uncle that it was a very good decision. "She needs to study, and she is an obedient child. Thank you for supporting me, my brother. May our ancestors keep you well and may my daughter thrive under your care."

"She will," my uncle had answered.

***

Uncle Modi's wife, Aunty Kiden, became my new mother. She bathed me, dressed me, and prepared me for school. As I became older, she supervised me. She fed me and told me stories of my homeland with the hope that one day, we would all go back home and reunite with our families.

Time flies, as they say. I made friends, I learned the language, and I forgot the pain. Soon I was a young woman in my uncle's household. My dark complexion defined me. My black kinky hair framed my face. My collar bones stood out with rage. My eyes popped out of their sockets in curiosity. I was a rather tall girl for my age. Uncle Modi did his best to feed me. He bought all kind of foods in the house, but I just could not tuck in any fats. He was not always around to monitor me, but was in and out, up and about, doing his business. I never grasped what exactly he did, as for months on end, he was absent from his own home. All I knew of him was that he loved to listen to the BBC and would unwind to the famed Congolese Lingala music that everyone back home enjoyed, including Papa.

I grew up in the care of his wife – Aunty Kiden and house maids who became a constant feature in my life. The maids would come and leave after a short time. Each house help brought a different character, a chapter and plot twist to my imaginary book about the happenings in that home. "They came, they helped, they went." That was my title.

"You know," Aunty Kiden told me one day, "This is your new home. You have to be strong and adapt well until the day we shall all return. You must stop starving yourself and eat so that when you return home, you can be a useful citizen. We were all born in our motherland, but we had to flee from the raging war. It is unfortunate and life is not easy in this place, but we must survive," Aunty Kiden said with a distant look in her eyes. She then told me the story of how she and uncle Modi met and how they ended up in Kenya.

\*\*\*

"The day we first met, your uncle Modi had decided to unwind from his day by coming for some tea at Malakia, the place where I worked. He stopped near my charcoal stove where I was squatting as I wafted the flames. I heard him ask for a cup of tea and I looked up at him. I swiftly straightened up and served him. I always had tea in the flask. After he took the tea, he said that I was smart. I smiled. I was dressed in my colourful jelebiya.

"From then on, Malakia became his daily tea spot. It was a residential area whose culture breathed religious tolerance with a blend of Sudanese and South Sudanese cultures and religious etiquette: dressing, eating and even speaking. The tea spots that lay under shady trees and along shop pavements were part of the landmark features accentuating the city. Uncle Modi said he felt they would pass for a tourist attraction. He would sit and watch the empty milk tins piled in pyramid shapes and boiling water evaporating into nothing. He would listen to the clinking of spoons against glass and the groups of men speaking about anything and everything, with the occasional shisha smoke accompanying their hot beverages.

"One fateful day, Uncle Modi cycled to Malakia and bought a handful of Tamiya - a delectable fiery vegetarian snack made of ground chickpeas formed into patties. The women fried the patties every day. As he was sipping his hot coffee, he caught sight of an old neighbour of his passing by – his name was Lofu. They both asked each other about how the other was doing. Uncle Modi said he had taken off during the crisis and that he had to make sure his family was safe before coming back to work. I was listening as they spoke. I was interested in the conversation because he was now my husband in a way. He added that he relocated them permanently to Kenya. The friend also told his story in an animated chat. Just then I noticed the gentleman sitting next to them clear his throat and sigh, his chest moving up and down. He moved his chair and faced the two men. 'So who do you think you are?' he interrupted them. I knew trouble was coming. The man shouted about people who were fond of running away whenever insecurity presented itself. Your uncle responded that he was like any other human who had a right to life and when given opportunity to save himself and his family, he would take it.

"The gentleman's eyes were red with anger. He raised his hoarse voice and said that it bothered him that such people could leave and return to South Sudan as they wished. A few curious individuals began to gather, their feet shuffling towards the direction of the tense scene, like bees to honey. They listened to the heated exchange as they hovered in a mixture of silence and whispers, nods and head-shakes.

"Your Uncle Modi couldn't speak anymore. He rose and walked towards the shouting man. The man stood up and lifted his hand. Pointing with a trembling finger at the two men, he cursed even louder. I could see Modi's breathing becoming more and more laboured as his chest rose and fell. He reached where the man stood, and they stood chest to chest. Everything happened in quick succession: a blow, a striking pain and a staggering body bleeding from the nose. The stranger was on the ground. He watched in shock as Uncle Modi stormed off leaving a stunned Lofu and a small crowd.

"You could not say that your uncle Modi was wrong. And you could not say the man lying on the floor was wrong. Anger piles and erupts when it cannot be bottled up anymore.

"A few days later Uncle Modi told me we were moving to Kenya. And now, here we are."

"Hmm," I responded.

"Yes. That is my story. Our story." Aunt Kiden said.

"Thank you Aunty Kiden. And have you ever been to Malakia since then?" I asked.

"No, I have not. But as you know, I go home regularly these days. A time will come when Uncle Modi too will go home and be at peace with it."

"True, I responded."

"And a time will come when your parents will come and take you back with them, so that you can live like family again."

"I believe you Aunty Kiden. I believe you. But for now, you are my mother and Uncle Modi is my father," I said to her.

That night, we sat together on her favourite hand-woven mat as we ate our dinner. Later I crawled into bed and left my door slightly ajar. I was listening to Lingala songs which my aunt was playing from Uncle Modi's collection. The songs held for me memories of Papa whom I was finding continuously hard to remember.

**Daughter of a Song Bull,** Acrylic and Oil on Canvas, *Nyareeta Gach.*

**Divide & Conquer,** Acrylic and Oil on Canvas, *Nyareeta Gach.*

**Lost Boys,** Acrylic and Oil on Wood Panel, *Nyareeta Gach.*

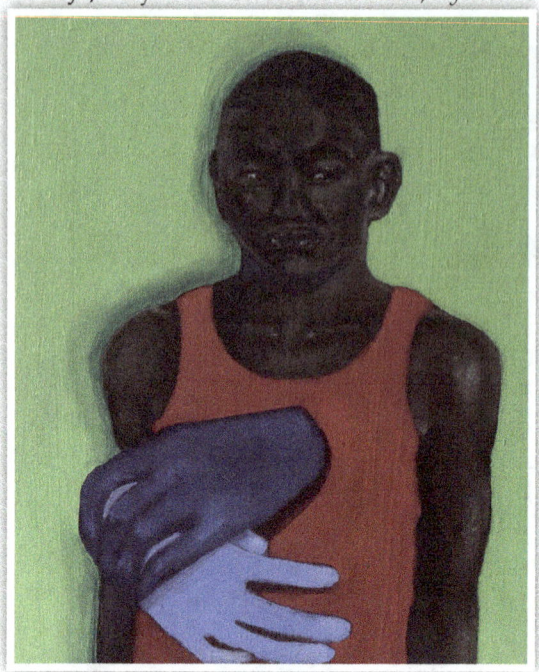

**Monopoly,** Acrylic and Oil on Canvas, *Nyareeta Gach.*

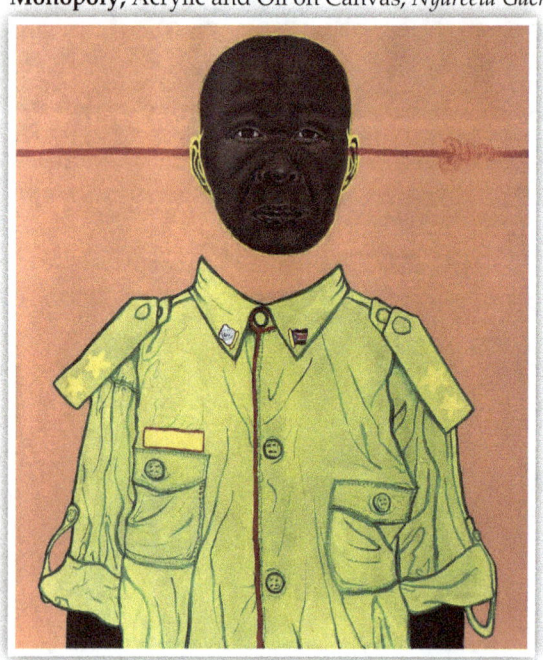

**Dashed Hope,** Coloured pencils on Art paper, *Degineyo Flavia.*

**M3 Legume sketch,** Gouache on paper, *Mare Lodu.*

**Self-Portrait,** Acrylic on Canvas, *Mare Lodu.*

**Malaan,** Inkjet Print on Archival Paper, *Atong Atem.*

**Adut,** Digital Print on Archival Paper, *Atong Atem.*

**Eva in flowers,** Inkjet Print on Archival Paper, *Atong Atem.*

**Nya,** Digital photography, *Ruth Nyaruot Ruach.*

**Dichotomy 2,** Digital photography, *Vonda Keji.*

**Not Just a hair style,** Offset paper with eco-friendly inks,
*Sunday Makuach*

**Untitled 1, Peace series,** Acrylic paint, *Abul Oyay*

**Untitled 2, Milaya Series,** Acrylic paint with beads and embroidery, *Abul Oyay*

**Untitled 3, My Plate of Combo Series,** Acrylic paint, *Abul Oyay*

**Untitled 4, My Plate of Combo Series,** Acrylic paint, *Abul Oyay*

**Untitled 5, My Plate of Combo Series,** Acrylic paint, *Abul Oyay*

**Untitled 6, Soldiers series,** Acrylic paint, *Abul Oyay*

**Untitled 7, Soldiers series,** Acrylic paint, *Abul Oyay*

*No Time to Mourn*

# Will my children cook and spice their little food in salsal tins?

*Nyibol Ajang Adier*

That day, sometime towards the end of 2005, we had so much fun. We spent most of the morning playing with other children from the neighbourhood. We gathered under our big mango tree and we were cooking food in small *salsal* tins emptied of their tomato paste. Because *salsal* tins are metallic, we used them to cook some of the *gadiya* leaves[26] we stole from our mothers' small cassava plantations. We used some of the onion remains from our mothers' kitchens. Sometimes we stole a few pieces of meat and sliced it into the *salsal* tins to add taste to our little food. Sometimes we pretended to be cooking but many times we prepared real food and ate.

My sister and I did not even have time to think about our mother and my brother who had been in the hospital for some days. My sister had accidentally hit my brother's hand with a pestle while she was pounding. Funny enough, when mother took the boy to the hospital, it was discovered that she too was sick and so they were both hospitalised for a while. This was our time to play as many games as we wished!

Yambio was a fun place. Everybody who came to play under the mango tree had a duty. Mine was to get fruits from up on the trees, because no one was better than me when it came to climbing. Not even any of the boys in the neighbourhood. I even used to climb papaya trees, weak as they usually are. My friends would wonder how the swaying papaya trees would hold my weight. "Make your body light," I would tell them. They would ask, "But how do you make your body light?" I would not know how to explain. All I knew was that you do not let the papaya carry all your weight. I would swing from one tree to the next just like

---

26    Cassava leaves in Zande language. The leaves are used to make sauce. It is a traditional food of the Zande people.

Tarzan, especially on the guava trees at the school's plantation. But truth be told, I used to be a tiny girl. But of course my climbing came with a lot of consequences. I would fall sometimes and get caned, but I still climbed any way. I would get caned in the morning and by afternoon, I would be up another tree. Climbing was something I couldn't resist because fruits were my food. Instead of getting a few fruits from down by shooting or plucking, I would rather climb and eat to my heart's content. One time I fell from a papaya tree and people thought I had died. They were shocked when I picked myself up, holding the big papaya I had plucked and fallen with.-

That day, my mom and my brother got discharged from hospital, disrupting our cooking. A few hours after they were discharged, some people came to our home. They were running and out of breath. "Thank God you are here and well. We thought you were still in the hospital. Look, war has come to us," they said to our mother. They told her that after she and my brother had just left the hospital everybody was attacked and slaughtered like chicken. "There were so many headless bodies and bodiless heads everywhere in the hospital compound and the vicinity. Maybe some people were slaughtered running, trying to escape," they said. How my mother and brother survived, only God could tell. We had been hearing people speak about war, but it had not reached Yambio.

Mother gathered my brother, my sister and me, and took us inside her hut. She dressed us in many clothes and tied cups around our waists just in case we split ways and needed to drink water along the way. She knew to do this because it was not the first time she was getting caught up in war. All her life, she had witnessed nothing but bloodshed during political and tribal wars. She had seen children starve to death and others die of thirst. She had seen parents die in wars and leave their children scattered. She herself was orphaned in war when her mother was shot in front of her. She told us that she got so traumatised, she wanted to remain with her mother's body, but nobody would let her. "You can't stay here," they told her as they dragged her off. "Let me bury my mother," she begged them. Nobody listened to her. She saw her mother die and saw herself being carried away without burying her mother. Only God knows whatever happened to my grandmother's body.

My mother faced a lot of challenges growing up without a mother. She knew the pains and hardships of families separated during war. She did not want that to happen to us, but she knew she had no control. "No one has control over war and in war," she always told us.

She packed all our household things and our clothes into bags and suitcases. Our home was surrounded by a fence of green shrubs that used to secrete a milk-like substance. Mother threw all bags and suitcases over the fence into the shrubs. She knew our grass-thatched houses might not survive the thirsty fires that had been said to consume homesteads similar to ours.

When the sky was starting to close her eyelids, we all huddled on my mother's bed. We wanted to end life together in case things did not turn out well for us in the night. My mother believed so much in God. She prayed the whole time while I, on the other hand, kept listening into the night in case anyone was outside. My brother and sister were sound asleep. What did they know? They were much younger. Mother is a very brave and hardworking woman. She, single-handedly, held us together through war. Our dad lived in another town, a different life all-together.

Later on in the night, there was a stampede outside. The whole village was awake. We could hear people running and shouting. We jumped out of bed and joined the crowd outside. We moved in the same direction that everyone else was taking. Along the way, gunfire opened behind us. It was so close that my mother pulled me into her bosom. If she hadn't done that, I would today be just a memory. The bullet passed close to my ear and it bruised the person who was in front of me. Some people got hurt by the bullets. One man was shot in the thigh, but someone helped tie his wound and he kept moving. I think these were stray bullets.

The funny thing about that night is that I never got scared, not even one bit. My mother had always told us about her war experiences and at some point it began to sound like just a story. That is how I felt as we run. I felt like we would return home to our normal lives the next day. Then every day became like that in my mind - I kept thinking that the following day we would go home and I would climb papayas one after the other. I guess that is how I managed to survive those hard times. Many children my age or younger, and others older, did not survive the tragedy. They went to be with the Lord, as my mother would say to me after each child would stop breathing and be carried away. Some of the children were my playmates either back at home or while on the run.

That first night on the run we kept moving from place to place in a zigzag direction to avoid the bullets behind us. Being in a large group made the situation more bearable. I knew we were not in this alone. But there was a bigger problem: the children. Yes, at eight years, I was a child too, but of course, many mothers had babies on their backs. Some of them cried with every gun shot, and others were already traumatized. The children kept crying and crying, forcing us to keep changing hiding places for fear of being discovered by the fighters. Sometimes we would think we had found a safe place to hide and start resting, but then the children would start crying and we would have to file out and start walking or running once again. I think we walked and ran for about two days straight. Or maybe it was just one night…I do not remember clearly.

When we finally reached a more secure place close to a church, we all sat down. No one was talking to each other. Everyone was staying alert, but we did not know what to say to each other. My back was aching because I had been carrying my little brother the whole time as we moved from one place to another. My mother carried my sister because she was a little heavier than my brother.

People were shocked that I was strong enough to run with my brother on my back, but what else could I have done? Leave my mother to run with two children? No. But I tell you, when danger is following you, you can run with a grinding stone on the head and you would not feel it until you put it down. I managed by God's grace. Some of my age-mates were scared and had to be carried. I was happy that on the contrary, I was brave enough not only to run on my own but also to carry somebody else.

To relieve my aching back, I sat down on the ground as soon as we stopped walking. The place was covered with tiny stones, the kind of stones usually found on un-tarmacked roads. That is where we slept. That night, comfort did not matter, all we were praying for was to be alive the next day. I removed the extra clothes I was wearing and laid them down for my sister to put her head on. My mother sat next to a wall, and I laid my head on her lap. My dear mother stayed up praying the whole night.

The following day we started moving again. We would not stay in one place because those fighting would always try to locate hide-outs and kill people. Days and nights passed and we were still walking, sleeping in bushes, eating only once in a while. The situation became unbearable but there was nothing else to do. We moved on. I missed home. We could not play. We could not have any fun. We could not laugh the way we used to back home even if sometimes we wanted to. We could not go to school. We could not enjoy anything. We did nothing else except walk, rest, and run. Maybe the days were not so many, but in my child's mind, they were countless.

At some point we found an abandoned bungalow and camped in it. It had several rooms and we were happy to find a roof over our heads although we slept on the floor. Later I learnt that the bungalows belonged to Arabs who had fled South Sudan during civil war. As days rolled on, we the children, began to loosen up a little. We started to play again, at first with only a few children around us and later more and more children joined in. This war had brought many of us together. We were many children from different villages. We all began to play together. We learnt new games from children from other villages. We played *borboru*[27] and *tungali*[28] and the boys played football. We began to reinvent our entire childhood because we realised the prospect of going back home had become distant.

I remember one night, I think it was a Wednesday, a man was brought to the bungalow. The bungalow was like a camp, but it was not a camp. People just reached there, stopped and lived. In war, any place becomes home for as long as it is safe and any home that is not, is abandoned. The man's leg was swollen. We later got to know that it was the same man who had been shot in the thigh on the first night. He was not receiving proper treatment. He was being treated with just herbs, warm water and salt. People were saying that 'poison' from the bullet had spread throughout his leg and into his body. The man could barely sleep at night. He would cry loudly, especially when his leg would be getting massaged. As children, we found his crying a bit funny because he had a very deep voice and would sound like a mooing cow.

Those days were horrifying. We read fear in the faces of the adults but pretended we knew nothing because there was nothing we could do about it anyway. The adults too pretended that we did not understand. They would go out and return with food and sometimes with a cow or a goat, kill it and distribute meat. We never asked where the food came from. Instead we sauntered away to play. I missed cooking in *salsals* because there were no *salsals* where we were. I missed climbing papayas. I missed being a child.

We would overhear our parents say to each other that our country was in a mess because of misunderstandings and tribalism, and that children and women were the most affected. We were forced to reflect on such complicated discussions at an

---

27    Dodge ball game
28    A children's game where they put twelve or six stones in a hole and keep running a short distance and returning to scoop the stones out of the hole.

early age. They talked about the so many orphaned children and widowed women, about the men suffering too, who died in war every now and then, about never learning from previous mistakes and clinging on to past actions that would never help us go forward as a nation. Even though on many occasions we were chased away when the adults were talking, we still heard a lot of burdensome stories that needed to be put aside.

As an adult now, I can't stop asking myself why on earth South Sudan hasn't borrowed a leaf from countries like Rwanda, for instance, with regard to how it solved its tribal issues. After the genocide in Rwanda, to this day, a Rwandan would never introduce themselves as Tutsi or Hutu. Now they are just Rwandan. Yet in my country, to get help, people need to know your tribe before they can help you. Where did we go wrong as a nation, what happened to the Comprehensive Peace Agreement (CPA)?[29] I ask because as a refugee, I no longer understand where we stand as a nation despite the agreements.

About one week after the wounded man had been brought to the bungalow, a helicopter and a lorry arrived at our bungalow. They must have come from the United Nations because that is what I remember seeing written on the tent-like structure on the lorry. They called people to get on to the lorry and in to the helicopter to be taken away. The rush to get on either was survival of the fittest. Knowing there was little chance for the four of us to all find space on the helicopter, my mother opted for us to run to the lorry. Indeed we got on and even found space to sit. Some man carried my brother, my mother sat on the opposite end carrying my sister and I sat next to her. When those who had gone to fight for the helicopter returned to join us, there was no more space. In my heart I was very grateful to my mother because if she had not been clever, we would have been the ones looking this way and that way, for where to put our bodies. As we drove away and the

29      The Comprehensive Peace Agreement (CPA) was signed to mark the end of the two-decade civil war in Sudan. It was signed in 2005 by the Sudan People's Liberation Movement and the Government of Sudan. Signing took place in Naivasha, Kenya. Cerebrations were at Nyao Stadium in Nairobi.

helicopter took off, I felt bad for those who had remained behind but there was nothing I could do to help. Fortunately, the people in charge had promised that there were two more lorries on the way and that the helicopter would return. I didn't know what fate had in store for them but neither did I have any idea where fate was taking us. I had hope that the wounded man would recover because by the time we left, his leg was looking much better and the swelling had reduced. But he never made it to the lorry nor to the helicopter on that day.

*** 

Today as I sit on top of the hill overlooking the road that leads north towards my country,
I wonder,
When will I go back home?
Will things ever be normal again?
Will traditional drums ever be heard again from the village square announcing dance competitions?

I ask God,
Whether children will run on Yambio streets to celebrate the Christmas season,
Whether they will eat dates and climb the mango trees of their own land?

I ask you, God,
Will my children cook and spice their little food in salsal tins?

# Battling with fear of the unknown

*Grace Wenepai Enosa*

The year was 1990. I will never forget that bright morning when my late husband and I woke up with a great plan for the day. We had just concluded a successful memorial ceremony for my mother and we were trying to relax after the occasion. I left my seven month old baby home with her father and went to buy some food in the market. I was planning a very nice meal. As I was walking by the roadside going to the market, I noticed the strange movement of military cars full of armed forces driving back and forth. When I arrived at the marketplace, there were only a few people there. I began to feel uneasy. I hurried to buy the things I needed and returned home to tell my husband about what I had seen.

My husband moved out of the house and went into the neighbourhood to inquire from other people what they thought or knew to be the problem. We had no telephone to call anyone or for anyone to call us, nor a television to watch news on. Our only means of communication were person to person and written letters. When my husband returned home, he told us that the situation was bad.

"What is the problem?" I asked him.

"I have no idea, but we must leave at once," he said.

"Where are we leaving to?" I asked again.

"You are asking too many questions," he said. "You will go with other people. They say they are moving to other towns. You will go to a nearby town with the children while I remain behind to monitor the situation. I will pick you tomorrow. It is not safe to remain here today."

When I noticed that he was serious, I packed a few things especially for the children since I knew I was returning the following day. We left our place and moved into town where we spent a night. I stayed awake, worried about my husband because there was continuous shooting throughout the night. Fortunately, he arrived very early in the morning and told us that the situation was critical and that even town where we were was very unsafe.

"We have to leave the town at once," he said.

"Okay," I said. I did not ask the same questions I had asked the day before because I could see horror on his face as he spoke.

We were many people in the place where we slept. Everybody started moving in all directions except the direction from which we had come the previous day. Some people forgot their own children. People created footpaths with their legs and bare hands through the thick forest. Others perished in car accidents out of panic. A lorry appeared and some of us jumped onto it. People just kept jumping onto the lorry without caring that it was too overloaded.

When the driver started the lorry to set off, I told my husband I want to come down because I was extremely uncomfortable. He told me that if I dared climb down, that would be the end of our marriage.

"Why," I asked him.

"Because I will not get down to be with you," he said. We all stayed on the lorry and kept quiet even when someone sat on our leg or stepped on our toes.

We had driven several kilometres from that town when suddenly the back door of the lorry opened on its own and some people fell out. Two people died on the spot while a few others got terrible injuries. The men picked the bodies and put them back onto the lorry. We thought we were overloaded before the accident. Now we had dead and bleeding passengers too.

The drivers tied the back door with rope and the lorry set off again. We were told that we were heading for the Central African Republic (CAR). Quietly I confessed my sins and said my last prayer to God. Anything was possible in this lorry. In these circumstances, anyone could die. I could be next. All the while, my seven-month-old baby was crying in my arms due to the pressure and heat in the vehicle, but there was nothing else I could do besides stay in that lorry. We moved the whole day. At night, when we finally reached the border, some of the men decided to bury the dead bodies. We crossed into CAR the following day.

This journey taught me many lessons. When I left my house, I did not know that it would be a final separation from things I thought were mine, from the great plan my husband and I had had the day before, and from the plans I had for myself and my family. Within two days, my world and dreams had crumbled and we were face to face with the unknown. We come with nothing to this world and we will take nothing with us. My eyes have seen terrible things in life, but God has kept me alive. The way we left our homes made me reflect on the end-times as spoken about in the Bible.

We were detained about six miles after crossing the border into the CAR. More vehicles arrived carrying more people. They mainly belonged to international organisations. We stayed at the border for almost six days, waiting for approval from CAR government. Remember we had left our homes with the idea of returning the following day. We had not taken enough food or other important things with us. All we had were a few clothes and blankets. The only thing we were surviving on was wild fruits from the forests. Crossing the border was a difficult task for drivers. It was a narrow road through a remote forest, mainly used by pedestrians. We walked our way to the police station while the drivers remained to struggle with the vehicles. This made things hard for us because we were not able to carry the children and all the things we had brought with us. Of course we left the things back in the vehicles.

While we were waiting for approval at the police station, we heard from the people who were continuing to arrive, that the soldiers had already reached the border town from where we crossed into CAR. They said there was heavy fighting and many people had been shot dead and left behind with no one to bury them.

We finally got the approval from the government and we were preparing to leave for the refugee camp the following day. That evening, I was bathing my children before putting them to bed when suddenly my husband came running and told me to run into the bush. When I looked behind him, I saw two military men chasing him. Apparently, as we were planning to leave the next day, the soldiers too were planning and had already made an ambush around us. Unfortunately, the CAR government had not deployed extra military to defend the border, so we were left to the mercy of God.

I had no energy to hold the kids, but thank God my elder sister was with me at the time. We had fled together. She took my three-year-old son and left me with my daughter in my arms. We ran as bullets rained behind us till we entered a thick forest. Thorns tore into our skin at ease, but we ran on. When we had gone deep into the forest we paused and listened. We did not hear any more bullets. It was then that we took a break. It was a thick, remote rain forest full of wild animals, where the only light was the few rays from the stars and moon that managed to penetrate the thick canopy of the tall trees. We sat down on the cold grass and leaves in the forest, battling with the fear of the dark unknown until the sun rose.

After failing to get us, the soldiers returned to Sudan that night with all the vehicles and our things in them. In the morning, we all emerged from our hideouts and assembled at the police station. We had no other option but to start walking immediately before other soldiers returned. We were told that sometimes soldiers pretended to go away then suddenly returned. We walked for three days till we reached the refugee camp.

To cut a long story short, exile ended in separation and divorce between my husband and me. He took away all our children and returned to South Sudan. I could not report anywhere or ask for custody because my husband was a Paramount Chief at the refugee camp and nobody could stop him from taking away the children. I stayed on my own in CAR. Life became very tough. After a while, I decided to try and give myself a new start. I met a man who seemed serious and responsible. I needed company too and so we started a relationship. I got pregnant and he seemed okay with that but unfortunately when I was only two months pregnant, he ran away leaving me to the mercy of God.

I struggled on my own through early pregnancy to full-term. I gave birth on my own and tried to forget that I ever had a partner. Life was so tough that I sometimes wondered whether I would make it to the next day. At some point I worked as a health agent for Africare, an American organisation. I did not just sit and wait for my situation to change. I was searching for opportunities everywhere. I searched for scholarships too because I felt I could go back to school. At some point I got a university address in a magazine on my boss's desk at Africare then I applied for scholarship. It was in the USA. It took only one month and I got a letter of acceptance to study but they had not given me a scholarship. I continued to try other options to no avail.

My daughter was four years when her father resurfaced. He apologised and begged for reconciliation. He said he had realised his mistakes and he asked for a second chance. He said he wanted to be with me so we could raise our daughter together, in a proper family. I was hesitant but I was in prayed and fasted, seeking God's direction. After consultations with fellow Christians and church leaders, I gave in. We stayed together and I could see that he had changed and was ready to settle down. It was during that time that I got pregnant again. I was two months pregnant when he ran away again and he never returned. Unfortunately for him, he passed away a few years later before he could experience the joy of fatherhood. I say that because I really love and enjoy my children today.

Sometimes we read the word of God but still have doubts when we are pressed from all sides by circumstances in life. We can easily get frustrated and angry about how things are in our lives. Most of us go through such times but we should be careful what we say or how we think because the Lord knows all about our struggles. One Thursday evening when I was getting ready to go to church for midweek service, it occurred to me that I actually no longer had clothes that fit. I had no money to buy new clothes. I was angry about my situation and I wondered why God gave me the second pregnancy when he knew the man would not take good care of me and my unborn baby?

I did not want to miss any service because church was the only place of hope for me. All around me, people were mocking my situation. The word of God was my only source of hope and joy. On my way to church I thought to myself: this is the last time I am going to church. I knew I would even be bigger the following Sunday. I arrived in the church and the service was great as usual. I was blessed by the word of God but still I was bothered by the fact that this was my last time till I would deliver.

When the service ended, one sister in the church came to me with a nylon bag in her hand.

"Sister Grace," she called me.

"Yes my dear," I responded.

"I thought of blessing you with some clothes since your stomach is now big," she said as she handed me the nylon bag, all the while smiling. I was speechless and I started asking God in my heart to forgive me. God knew my thoughts, my struggles, and my doubts and he had appointed someone to bless me with just what I needed the most.

Those days I saw the hand of God move into our lives in a spectacular way. There is one evening when my daughter came to me crying because of hunger. She was three years old. I had nothing to give to her. I held her in my arms and comforted her until she slept. After she slept, I felt angry and began to complain to God. I told God it was better for me to die and let someone else take care of my daughter than to watch her misery. I was awake for so long complaining to God. By around midnight a verse from the

Bible popped up into my mind: "It is written: that man shall not live on bread alone, but on every word that comes from the mouth of God."[30] I started saying these words in prayer and suddenly I felt something strange on my tongue and I started to speak like a baby and felt heavy power all over my body. I felt at peace and slept until morning.

Early the following morning someone was knocking at my door. When I opened, I found my friend`s husband was at my door. I welcomed him in, gave him a seat and he started praying. When he finished, he told me that in the night, the lord told him to pay his tithes to me but he did not understand why because he always took his tithes to his pastor in the church but the voice kept telling him to bring the money to me. He gave me the money and left, I remained speechless and grateful to God. Surely His mercies are new every morning. God is with us at our lowest point in life, He is also with us at our highest. He hears us when we cry and also when we complain, when we are weak and when we are strong. He is our father.

One Sunday morning I was closing the door to go to church and the landlord confronted me for house rent. I did not know how to calm him down, but I told him I would pay the rent when I returned from church. I was in a hurry because I was in the choir and needed to be in the church for rehearsal before the service started. I left for the church without knowing how I was going to pay the rent because I had no money, not even for my next meal. As I was walking going to the church, I heard a voice telling me, "How do you expect to get the money in the church to pay the rent as you just told the landlord? Just go to the marketplace and ask people for money." But in my heart, I did not want to miss the service. I told myself that I would go to ask people after I return from the church.

The service was awesome: the worship session, the preaching and simply being in the presence of God. It was a powerful time with God but towards the end of the service, I had

30      Matthew 4:4.

second thoughts about going to the market. I asked myself what I was going to do once the service was over. I thought I should go and stay with a friend and then return home in the night when the landlord would be asleep.

When the service was over, the pastor left the hall and went to his office. We remained in the choir singing as people left the building. Before I left the building the pastor sent someone to take me to his office. When I got to him, he gave me an envelope and told me, the elders in the church had had a meeting the day before and approved some money for my house rent and feeding. With tears in my eyes, I thanked God for His faithfulness. I had not told the pastor about my situation but I had prayed to God and He heard me and provided from the church account. The question is, what if I followed the voices that told me to go and beg in the marketplace? Why didn't the landlord ask me for rent on Saturday and instead he asked on Sunday? God is still doing miracles in our time!

***

When my contract with Africare ended, life at the refugee camp became unbearable. I decided to try the American Embassy for sponsorship for the university that had earlier admitted me. I travelled to Bangui, the capital city of CAR, to look for some possibilities. That was also another journey of unknown journeys. I had no relatives in Bangui and no money. I only moved with faith in God. My daughter was two years old by the time I moved. When I reached the embassy, they told me that it was difficult to get sponsorship together with my daughter who was two years by that time. They however referred me to UNHCR and they recommended me for a resettlement program that was taking place at the time.

I was interviewed by an agent sent from Geneva. It took me three years to get a response and get resettled to Norway. During the interview, I had informed UNHCR of my three children who had returned with their father to South Sudan. Before I departed from CAR, UNHCR informed me that I had the right to take with me 10 people listed as family members on the resettlement form. I was happy that I was finally going to reunite with my children.

I relocated to Norway in 2003. As soon as I got there, I started the process of bringing the children. Their father had passed away and they were on their own. I was shocked when the immigration office in Norway dodged the case and only one of my children was allowed to join me, still after a long struggle. It is sad that the Norwegian immigration office has continued to reject my children's applications for visitor visas to come to Norway and visit. My children have not enjoyed close brotherly love because of the immigration restrictions and useless wars. It has been difficult supporting and taking care of my scattered family.

Like thousands of other South Sudanese, I continue to live away from South Sudan. My son was six months when we moved to Norway. He will turn 18 in December 2020. I miss my older children who live in other parts of the world, but they are now grown up and with their own families.

When Nowhere Has Felt Like Home

# Home in Flames
*Lydia Minagano Kape*

A mother's hug
Is a child's heaven
A fresh breeze from green gardens?

Where do you turn to when her body is in flames
When home is a burning bush
But our knees cannot go down to worship
Because this fire is not holy?

Would you leave
To save your life?

It is hard to build a home away from home
We tried,
But we are stuck in other lands
Lands that do not know how to pronounce our names
Strangers we remain
However much we twist our tongues
Sometimes, we miss a vowel, or the silent letters
It is hard to build a home away from home.

Would you stay
To put out the fire?

But what do you do
When you pour the Nile to extinguish the fire,
While others feed it oily wood from our forests?

When home burns to ashes?
What do you do?

# My family abroad
*Kaka*

My family abroad lives on an island.
My father once called it a prison on water,
Where everyone must pay to live, must pay to breath
And must be reminded everyday of how lucky they are.
My family abroad lives in luxury, the luxury of nothingness.
They left in war,
They took with them what they could carry: a handful of kids.
A successful day for my family abroad is when after yelling and
screaming:
"Hello?"
"Hello."
"Hello, can you hear me?"
"Hello."
"Hello, I hear you. Can you hear me?"
"It is poor network. Your voice is faint, but I hear you."
"How is everyone? Here we are doing fine."
"Everyone is sick, the old woman is… everyone is weak."
"Okay. Government will pay me in a week. I will send send the
help."
Bills pile
They ring like the phone tone.
Put it up there, right on top of the other overdue bills, I will pay it
when next *Centrelink*[31] pays.
Up on top of the water bill, the electricity bill, the housing bill…
My family abroad and my family at home are attached to
government like a child to a tit.
A successful day is when we are happy hearing each other's voice

---

31      Australian Government program that provides services and payments,
including welfare

# My telephone Dad

*Kaka*

My telephone dad likes to remind me he is my father.
I link his voice to his words to his breath.
My telephone dad thinks yelling on the phone works.
My telephone dad tells our arranged mum how to raise us.
How to keep us in order.
He tells her what he wants us to know.
To learn,
To study,
To marry.
That is my telephone dad.
Our telephone dad is funny,
He deploys his bass over the phone as if we should know he's put
his foot down.
We could choose not to listen to him, after all he is just on the
phone,
He likes to remind us of how much he sacrificed by sending us
abroad.
How hard he worked to pay this and that tuition.
All that while on the phone.
My telephone dad wanted a doctor, he got a nurse.
He wanted a lawyer, he got a therapist.
Wanted a successor, he got resentment from his son.
My telephone dad does not understand
Why his sons do not know what it takes to be a man of the house.
He does not understand why his sons do not understand him.
Yet he's told them everything over the phone.

# My mother arranged

*Kaka*

My mother arranged mothering and fathering seven kids for
thirteen years abroad.
She arranged telephone calls to enable our father to father us over
telephone.
She arranged for the roof over our heads.
For food on our table.
For English on our tongues.
My mother arranged for work with no English.
Our arranged mother spoke to us in Dinka; our father's language.
For ten years, our mother arranged for us to learn two languages
while she forgot her own.
With no English on her tongue she arranged for her seven kids to
go to school.
She arranged parent-teacher interviews and we translated what
they said to her and she to them.
We read school forms, reports and letters to her and
she arranged her signature when needed.
My mother arranged.

# My Aunty

*Kaka*

My aunty works in a freezer.
She works to feed her sister at home, her daughter in her room, a
son at the gym.
My aunty hardly sleeps.
My aunty has never known poverty.
She lives in memories of childhood wealth
Back in the village
Back at home
Back in her mind.
My aunty works hard, the bills work harder, home illnesses work
harder.
My aunty worked so hard, she developed a tumour in her heart
Diagnosed to be caused by allergies.
She brushed it off her shoulder,
She went back to work
Because what is allergies to bills on top of bills, on top of bills?
She cannot complain of poor work ethics in the fridge.
Cannot complain of pain in her back nor blindness in her eye.
She cannot see poverty because she sees a job.
When she goes to *Centrelink* for welfare pay, they yell their
English at her.
She smiles.
They tell her to go to school.
She can't because English will not pay bills.
My aunty has enough English to go by.
Enough to work in the fridge
To recognise that the response to;
*"Hi, how are you today?"* is always: "Good."
Enough English to say chai.
When she gets home from work, she lies down on the couch in
the kitchen.

By the time the tea arrives, she is in slumber land.
My aunty smiles in her sleep.
She has a job.

## Diaspora
*Bigoa Chuol*

12,505 kilometres of grief
Sorrow for what you do not remember
Palpable loss
For faceless people that have vanished

Places, you've never seen
We live with the residue of home
They have squandered the point of belonging

Its mourning fragments
Torn and stolen things

Memories that are delicate
That cannot be made whole
Because they are borrowed
From those who borrowed from others before them
Who borrowed from buried things
From silence

We do not know if it is possible to know a place
Or how to call it yours
When nowhere has felt like home
You're not quick to put your roots in the ground

Daughter,
These borrowed memories remain
But may have not much
Left to give you.

# Essence

*Chudier Pelpel*

They want to know the horror of my people's stories.

About the tribal warfare,
the famines.

The exploitation of millions
for resources their lands produce
but cannot fathom.
True gems are in the essence of people
not backwards.

Most are not interested in mining minds.

# This place
*Emmanuella Baker Ayul*

This place is confusing
It makes you feel weak
In the sense that you have no control.
Involuntary
that's what our whole lives are,
No power over situations
no guidance by choice.
Try to block out the noise
And see through the fuzziness,
the cloud that surrounds your mind
like an asteroid belt, it's chaotic.
It's like being a prisoner in your own mind.
Imagine a merry go round that won't stop moving, the same song playing.
Every time you hear the melody, it gets more and more irritating, louder and louder
like a ticking bomb ready to go off.
On till one day you get used to it and it's just an echo but it's still there.
Being in this place you feel like you've been drained of human emotion
the only thing you feel is melancholy.
You're in solitary confinement but you're the prison guard.
It's you versus yourself.
It's not always loud in there
sometimes it's quieter than a mouse,
so quiet your organs can be heard performing like an orchestra.
A heart valve snapping lub-lub causing a beat to echo,
air whistling as it goes through the wind pipes and into the lungs...

This doesn't last long…. but
in that moment you are thinking of nothing and everything at the
same time.
A place cluttered with emptiness and a ruckus,
like you are in a cabin, in the woods,
surrounded by a pack of hungry wolves
but you don't care if they break in.
And sometimes the wolves are your friends…and you feed them
bits of your flesh
till you are nothing but skin, bones and carcass.
They sometimes say cabin fever can kill you
but what if you never want to escape, and you've made that cabin
your home,
turned it into a fun house
there are no evil clowns or monsters because every day you look
in the mirrors
you are the bearded lady in your own freak show
no audience, just you and yourself.

# War times are war times

*Monica Animbue*

When my mother was a young woman and in school, her ambition was to become a Catholic nun. Her performance in school was excellent and based on that, the Catholic Church requested her parents to allow them to take her to Juba for further studies so that they could help her fulfil her dream. My grandmother did not want her to become a nun because my mother was the only daughter to my grandparents. Her daughter becoming a nun would mean that she would cease living with the family and would, of course, not get married in the future. Grandmother wanted grandchildren from her only daughter.

My grandfather, on the other hand wanted his daughter to fulfil her dreams and so he used his authority to arrange with the priests to take my mother. Grandmother learnt of the plan but she kept quiet. When the day came for my mother to go, my grandmother did not leave the house even for a second. My mother said that she probably did not even eat or drink for fear of nature's call. When the vehicle to take mother arrived, grandmother looked at them like she did not know what was happening. Mother had no choice but to come out of the house and board the vehicle. Grandmother jumped out of the house and lay on the ground in the middle of the road all the while swearing that her daughter was not going anywhere.

"You will crush me to death before you take her," she said.

"But this is for the good of your daughter," the church leaders who had come to take her pleaded.

"I know God's will," she told them. "This is my only daughter. Which God would want to take the only child away from her parents?" she asked, and refused to leave the road. When they saw that she was not ready to negotiate, the church leaders decided to leave without my mother.

Frustrated, my mother stayed in Yambio. Unfortunately, her parents were not able to continue paying her school fees. She dropped out of school after primary seven and got married to my stepfather, Musa Zande, who was from Tambura, close to the border with the Central African Republic. He lived in Yambio town. In a few years, she had given birth to my elder sister Juliana Nunu and my brother Joseph Kobila. She then decided to go and visit her parents and take them the children as was the Azande tradition. When a woman marries and has children, she is expected to take a break to visit her parents' home so that the parents see and bless the children.

Mother had just reached her parents' home when the war between the SPLM and the Khartoum establishment reached Yambio. That was in 1990. It was sudden and unexpected. My mother and her two children were forcefully separated from her husband. She could not manage to cross back to her marital home and did not even know whether the husband had stayed or fled his home, or even if he was still alive. She stayed alone as a single mother for almost six s. All her efforts to trace his whereabouts were futile. She sent messages to Tambura and everywhere else where she suspected him to be. She asked whoever she thought could have knowledge of his whereabouts but there was no trace of him. After some time, she was convinced that he must have died. Many people were dying: of hunger and starvation, of disease, by bullets, spears and machetes.

It was in this confusion that I came along. She had lost hope, was lonely and had two children to look after. She got into a relationship with another man and she became pregnant with me. He was ready to marry her but when my grandparents learnt of the pregnancy, they were not happy because she was still legally married to her husband. My grandparents refused my father's marriage proposal since there was nothing to confirm that my stepfather was dead. My mother lived in uncertainty, but nobody understood her situation.

Fortunately, a few months later, the war eased down. People who had run away from Yambio started returning. They talked about those who had survived and those who had died, those who had married and those who had abandoned their families. One day a refugee from DRC visited Yambio and he talked about a man he was with in DRC, whose wife was from Yambio. As it turned out he was talking about my mother and my stepfather. He told her that her husband was still alive and was a refugee in DRC. She was so happy to hear about him, but she was not sure of what to do since she was pregnant with another man's child. She told him that she had tried to find him and had given up. The man told my mother that my stepfather too had tried to reach my mother without success. "When you go back, tell him that you saw us," my mother told the stranger. When the man returned to DRC, he informed my stepfather that his wife and his children were alive and well in Yambio.

My stepfather immediately wrote a letter to my mother and asked her to join him in DRC. He sent someone to Yambio to get her and take her to DRC. My mother accepted. After all, her parents had not allowed her to get married to my father. When she arrived in DRC and my stepfather learnt of the pregnancy, he did not mistreat her. He understood the situation that had led to her pregnancy. In the meantime, he too had married another woman after he failed to trace my mother. My stepfather took on his wife and left the woman that he had married. That is another story.

About three months to delivery, my mother travelled back to South Sudan. Maybe she did not want her baby to be born in DRC. After I was born, we stayed for a short time with her family then my stepfather relocated from DRC back to Yambio town. He approached his in-laws and requested for his wife back and he accepted me and raised me as his daughter. He did not even want others to know that I was not his real daughter. i was told that he used to get angry at anyone who mentioned that I was a daughter to another man. I grew up knowing he was my father and I loved him as much. I still love my stepfather. It even makes me guilty calling him stepfather because he is the father I have known all my life. My biological father too was a very good man and so was his wife. I was blessed to have two loving fathers.

My mother reminds me that when I was about five years, I got seriously sick. I started coughing and the cough would not go. My parents took me for treatment, but I did not improve. I was checked for tuberculosis and it was negative. They tried everything but nothing worked. In the end when doctors were defeated, they said it was a chronic cough that was not treatable. Fortunately, I never transmitted it to my siblings, but I suffered a lot.

One day, my step-parents received a message from my paternal grandparents. They told them that the reason I was sick was because she had not taken me to visit them. They said it was their anger making me sick, and that I would die if my parents did not let me go to them fast. At first my stepfather refused to comply. It was during this confusion that I got to understand that my father was not my father. When I eventually visited, grandmother boiled a concoction of herbs and gave them to me. Interestingly, the cough subsided. From then on, each time the cough came, I would go visit, take grandmother's concoction, and get well.

We were beginning to settle in Yambio when we started hearing rumours that the Lord's Resistance Army (LRA) was coming to attack. Some people fled, but father said we should not run. He was tired of running. We remained home. One evening we were at home and we heard people entering our compound. It was the LRA soldiers. They dragged all of us out of our rooms and immediately put my father at gunpoint. They started hitting him and asking him to give them drugs, but we had nothing like drugs at home. My father fought back and we all joined in to rescue him. One soldier hit me on the neck and I still have pain from it. I bit his hand with all the strength I could gather. When he released me, I ran and hid in bushes behind the house. I sat the whole night without ever closing my eyes.

In the morning when I returned home, I knew there would be a dead body because I had heard gunshots in the night. Fortunately, my stepfather was alive. He told me that they had hit him several times and shot at him, but the bullet only bruised him. They had, however, thought him dead and had run away with my brother and mother.

The Arrow Boys[32] pursued the LRA rebels for seven days but then they gave up. One day we were at home and we saw my mother and brother walk in. They had swollen legs and wounds from the beatings. They told us that the rebels tied all of them to each other and if any of them got tired and failed to walk, they would be beaten. We were so happy to receive them back as some people never made it home.

But war times are war times. In Yambio, there were many people who were homeless after running from village to village. One day a woman approached my father and asked him to help her with a small piece of land where she could build a temporary shelter for her children. She was a single mother. My stepfather was a kind man. He took pity on her and apportioned part of his plot of land to her to stay. She built and started raising her children. One day the woman came home with the authorities. They had come to demarcate the land and create a boundary between her and my father. She claimed that it was her land. In war time, there is lawlessness. It seems the woman had bribed her way to take the land.

That evening my father asked me to go and buy for him his usual beer. As he and my mother drank, he told her that he was in shock over the betrayal. Mother said that the whole country was in a state of betrayal. They laughed and continued to drink, sending us for more and more drinks. As children we did not understand most of their conversations.

In the night we were all asleep when I heard stepfather knocking on my door. I was afraid and surprised, but I rushed to

---

32    Local South Sudanese youths especially from Western Equatoria region who organised themselves into a self-defense unit for their communities.

the door to find him lying helplessly on the floor, unable to walk. His right-hand side was paralyzed. He had not woken up mother because she had gone to bed drunk. I woke her up and I ran to inform the rest of the relatives. Interestingly, none of the relatives I informed came that night. They all came in the morning with a multitude of advice about what he should do to get well. Some relatives said he was bewitched by the woman he had quarrelled with while others said it was a stroke. They took him to different hospitals, but he did not get well. Some relatives went to medicine men and brought herbs; they did not help even though they cost him a lot of money. He would be on the verge of giving up when another relative would suggest another medicine man who, so they would say, had more potent medicine. Because he was in so much pain, he kept agreeing to go. I was the only child with him as all my siblings had been sent to school in Uganda. So I would move with him. At one time, I stayed with him at a medicine man's home for almost a month. He began to improve and even started walking, though with difficulty.

That medicine man was tricky. At some point he said that the medicine he was going to give the patient must be prepared and administered by a woman. There was no other woman except me. The condition was that I had to remove my rosary, my necklaces, bangles, waist beads and shoes before preparing the medicine. I removed everything except my rosary. The man became angry with me, saying the medicine would not work if I did not comply. I did not. He dragged me to where the medicine was and he started singing as if he was possessed by spirits. I did not care. When the medicine was ready, I gave it to my father.

When I came out and told people outside that I had refused to remove the rosary, they said I should never disagree with a medicine man. "Those people are witches," they said. "He could even kill you." I did not believe them. In the time I had spent at his house, I had learnt a lot about him. I knew he wielded fear and not power.

What I never told anyone was that the medicine man tried to rape me. He asked me to sleep with him many times, but I always told him I would scream if he attempted to rape me. Fortunately, there were always people in his home, my father inclusive. That is how I survived. But I can imagine what he would do to women and children who feared him. I did not tell anyone from my family about the rape threats. Not even my best friends. I did not want to create more problems in our home.

My father's situation worsened and he was taken to Juba for treatment. After one month he returned to Yambio, no better. He went to another herbalist in Makpandu and stayed there for another month, but there was no change. When he returned home, he abandoned all efforts and waited for his death. All relatives abandoned him. It was only my mother and I who looked after him. Sometimes my mother would get so frustrated and drink, leaving me alone to make all decisions. When one of our neighbours died, my father called me to his side and told me "I will be the next person to die in this area." My father did not live long after that. He died in 2009. There was a lot of talk about witchcraft and how we would all die like him if we did not go through cleansing rituals. We never did and we never died!

After his death I stayed with one of my uncles and he paid my school fees although the wife was not happy about it. In war, people scramble for resources. Many people are stingy not because they are mean but because there is so much pressure on the minimal resources. Eventually my uncle sent me to study in Uganda in 2010. I was put in Primary Five, which I had already completed in 2008 in Yambio. They said that the education system of South Sudan was at a lower level than that of Uganda. Unfortunately, my uncle lost his job shortly after that move. A wife to another uncle tried to help and was paying from her pocket money. She could not sustain that either! I dropped out again. I was called back to Yambio because my grandfather had passed away. After the burial, I started staying with my brother. Year after year I hoped someone, like the Good Samaritan, would appear and take me back to school, but those were just dreams. After a while I decided to get married. I felt like no one loved me or cared about me. Getting a husband would at least give me a friend. I married because of the situation I was going through.

I met my husband in Yambio in 2012 and we started dating. Shortly after that he moved to Kampala. About four months later I joined him in Kampala. In 2013 we returned to Yambio, but my brother ordered him to be arrested, claiming that he had kidnapped me. He spent a day in a police cell and got bailed out, but he still had to pay a fine. In the meantime, I got pregnant. Our first baby was born on 02/03/2014. My husband asked my people for my hand in marriage. They accepted and told him how much bridewealth he would have to pay, for the marriage to proceed. We were happy at last! However, when he asked them to allow us wed, they refused because he had not actually completed paying that money. In South Sudan, bride-wealth is such a strong tradition. Today we have three children, two girls, Naomi and Cicilia and one boy, Moses, but we still cannot regularise our marriage until he has paid every coin of that money. That is how it is for most young couples. Tradition does not know the difference between home and exile.

Our people say that once you have been attacked by a lion, whenever you hear one roaring, you block the door with heavy loads. That is what happened to us in January 2016. We were home and we heard that the Arrow Boys were preparing to attack and fight the Lord's Resistance Army of Uganda and the national army. The army barracks in Yambio was only three kilometres from our house. The army retaliated by burning houses of Azande people and killing them. We had no money at all but Kiera Chapman, a friend to my husband who lives in UK, led a crowd-funding campaign and sent us the money which enabled us to flee from Yambio to Juba and finally to Uganda. We reached Uganda on 14/01/2016.

Some people are very unkind to refugees. The situation of a refugee cannot be envied at all. In Uganda, we stayed with my sister-in-law but we were a burden to the family. My husband had no job and no source of income. We were very fortunate that my mother-in-law was in Norway and could support us at least with money for rent and feeding for a short while. I became pregnant with my second child, Moses, but towards delivery, my sister-in-law left for Arua. We were very worried but luckily, I had a safe delivery. Jesuit Refugee Service (JRS) stepped in and supported us for three months. The July 2015 conflict in Juba created an influx of refugees to Uganda, so JRS stopped their support. Life became extremely difficult as we sometimes survived on very little food.

My husband supported me to train in craft-making. I learnt how to make beaded bags, wallets, necklaces and earrings. I started making craft items and selling them to South Sudan. I taught my husband to make some of the items and we opened an online shop with Etsy and started selling the bags to Europe. I remember a day when we made a big sale of US$ 600. We used it to help us grow the business.

My husband has also initiated projects to help unaccompanied refuge children in Bidibidi refugee settlement. He himself suffered at one point as an unaccompanied refuge child. The idea for the project came after he read about unaccompanied children having difficulties in the camp and humanitarian organizations finding it hard to handle them. His approach is to help by engaging the children in social and musical activities and to train them with some life skills.

Although life remains difficult as we still struggle to pay school fees for our children, pay rent and buy food, we continue to work together. I am ready to support him too in this initiative because many children continue to be separated from their parents by death and by borders. Though I stopped school in Primary Five, I want to go back and study. I have heard about adult education. I believe that someday if I find a way, I will go back to school. You never know. My hope is alive.

# Conflict of Identity

# The scar

*Layet Busena*

Dear Mom,
If I were to meet you now,
I would ask whether I was really born of love,
Or survival.
I would ask you why you called me Layet.
Like a scar, the name Layet stands out.
See,
I have no memories of us,
Except questions.
Layet – dark hearted?
I know you tried to give me roses.
The beautiful multi-colour dresses from throw-away pieces of
village tailors.
The strong baby-carrier from Baba's old trousers...
Tell me, what kind of marriage did you have?
Love-filled?
Circumstantial?
Baba says you were 16 years old.
He says you two ran away from your families.
Was it loneliness that made you embrace in the forest?
And now,
Baba cries all the time when I ask about you.
He does.
He turns his face away when I ask.
Do you know why?

# Wide gap between your teeth

*Bigoa Chuol*

kɛl[33]      my mother is hard things,
beneath she has infused *teak* splinters cautiously
      mimicking leathery skin
    she is heavy,    it has flattened her feet
toughened women do not soften,
               they rust

    rɛw[34]
    my mother *is* rough handling,
      she says it shapes prudent daughters
livid, when it just presses them    wider and away

diɔk[35]    she insists,
  the water *piḫw*[36]   is the most exquisite
    and profoundly sweet in *Manchom* [37]
she means the memories,    her favourite brother is the one
    with the big gap between his top front teeth,
  like our *guandɔŋ* [38]    grandfather
    she declares they look most
alike when unbowed by
           calamity
this is when she speaks    about *nhök*[39]  about love,
  she loves him obscured by expanding  kilometres,
by gaps    as wide as between both

---

33      kɛl means number one in Thok Naath language of South Sudan. Ten stanzas begin with numbers: 1 to 10
34      rɛw means, two
35      diɔk means, three
36      *piḫw* means, water in Thok Naath language
37      *Manchom* Village in South Sudan
38      *guandɔŋ* means, grandfather
39      *nhök* means, love

their top front teeth


ŋɔaan[40]

in 1997, we nuzzled into each other
and took photographs in front of all the
*bougainvillea*
in Nairobi
our favourite is the purple and pink
that april, head outside window     on a sunday,
vomit washed back onto the side of the *matatu*
the conductor insisted          my mother clean it
I now try to sleep when I feel nauseous
Inter-generational gaps are mature potholes
we will not arrive
cleanly


dhiẹẹc [41]          when father is murmuring in the night,
I find a birthday card
from my mother's brother, dated the year
1997
this one,          they look most alike in the hair
In their *sorghum* sized coils
he is fifth sibling and she is fourth but
he has no gaps     in all his clean straight white
teeth
she compliments his gums,
they are a pale pink *bougainvillea*


bakɛl[42]

we presume *guandɔŋ*
has not noticed the language     collapse
in the mouths of his grandchildren,

---

40     ŋɔaan means, Four
41     dhiẹẹc means, five
42     bakɛl means, six

*No Time to Mourn*

              dispatched
to back molars to be chewed
                          occasionally
    we hope he thinks of *us*
          when he is weaving trinkets,
we hope there is some left to return
          home when we visit    very soon
    It hurts his hands      nowadays
they beg him to slow down       they mean stop


barɔw[43]        your smile is a collision
your mouth is
                  catastrophe with      teeth
I am 17 years old; she asks me to       explain
why I want to leave the house when my father died
      only two years ago


        ba̱de̱k [44]
my brave        brother boy, his tears fall faster
than he can ball his hands into fists
    weep,              mourn
      reaches out to embrace
quicker than he can implode into rage
      *recipe* to compelling
                    softness
he looks like Baba,      therefore, graduates first sibling
          an arch for flat feet


              ba̱ŋɔan[45]  come home and see the *okra*
bloom flowers,    clip *guandɔŋ's* toenails
      and stroke his white hair      with a *soft* comb
          he laughs with his spirit

---

43        ba̱rɔw means, seven
44        ba̱de̱k means, eight
45        ba̱ŋɔan means, nine

quells our casual      scepticism with delicious kindness,

            *spit* and     ceremony

puɔhth[46]

     there are no children here of a lesser

        god


                         weḻ[47]

           there is rest,

snatch it from the       kilometres expanding

    prepare the place we can lay

   mother *sleep* long

       *sleep* long     till

           your sides *hurt*

---

46       puɔhth means, blessing
47       weḻ means, ten

          *No Time to Mourn*

# Identity

*Apeay Ogeli*

this is I and I am this
melanin-rich skin so deep
spiritually awakened to the highest vibrations
frequencies aligned from time to time
a balance between two worlds
unfolded
between God and the devil
between babylon and heaven
divine intervention
I don't think they understand the message
we are captivated by the wrong things
while they take and take and watch us break
speak to your ancestors
they hold the truth
look within you
retrieve your value
it was never lost
it was hidden

# I Am Afraid

*Kiden Jackline*

I am afraid to return
To a place I called home
Because if I do, I am afraid
I'll lose all I've got
What's left of me
My life.

I am afraid of those who stirred the storm
Leaving me live on the run like a fugitive
With no place to call home.

My home
Of intoxicated air
Where blood floods across the land
Gun powder filling up lungs
Chocking.

I fear not death
But having no one to listen to me
Anyone able or strong.

I am afraid of remorse,
Of bodies left to decompose on the streets
Of streets, filled with the blood we know.

I am afraid of uncertainty
Of the day that would unfold if I spoke
Of those who robbed me of family
Those who robbed me of identity
Would anyone hold them accountable
When I am gone?

*No Time to Mourn*

Everyone is a victim of the next victim
We were not born like this
We are a product of the system
Where we lost our relevance
Broken spirits of decadence

Afraid I am because I am afraid.

# Bicultural Lens

*Grace Akon*

My mother says Khartoum would hold me like a star.
I see flashes of a could-have-been life.
But here I am, writing about the home I never got to have.
What would life be if war never touched my home?

Here,
I think of myself as two different women.
An aftermath of survival.
A testament of mother's will.

We live life constantly aware of our skin.
It is after all what drove us from Sudan.
Though it's been years,
I can still see the glint in my people's eyes.

Maybe home is running from the thing that hates you.
Fleeing the arms of a country that wants to kill you,
Into another whose intentions,
You cannot read.

America is always rubbing into the wounds of my healing family.
And someone told me the other day, that if I don't like America I
should go back to Africa.
Yet I've been trying to write myself into a free woman in both,
A flaming star in both.

No matter where I go I am always currency.
Bought, distributed,
Always, always,
At a profit.

# To Everyone who has Laughed at my Dinka

*Grace Akon*

I want to tell you,
That I once knew how to speak this language;
Dinka.
Now I am scared of opening this mouth
In fear of getting laughed out of the room.

My tongue
Is always searching for its lost home.
Stumbling and falling.
Broken

Maybe it happened when my first language turned second.
When the words that once flowed like water turned honey-thick
slow.
When I had to pose and think,
Before I could speak,

I want to tell you,
My Dinka is the dead plant I keep watering, in hopes of bloom.

# Therapy for stained infants

*Veoulla Baker Ayul*

Can't you see that the same pain within me is the same as one within you? Mine is just much easier for people to view. There is no need to play, my frustrations are put on constant display, as murder, theft and hate shared across the globe for people to commentate.

You don't have to look far to figure out why we're the way we are. All the injustice and crime, people haven't done their time, thanks to those in authority, who crippled minds.

Ours, both mine and yours.

Our nature has been polluted. Tradition has blinded us from what we envisioned.

They talk too much but never arrive at a decision.

They feign knights in shining armour to your rescue. When we look away, they put their swords in your back. If you ask, they say: "What did we do?"

Do not try to alter my brain. I am not insane, Spill your thoughts and here they remain.

A stain.

# Abyei Streams

*Alith Cyer Mayar Cyerdit*

I am the granddaughter,
Of the ancestors
Showered with bullets and bombs along Abyei streams.

The granddaughter of the forgotten land
Of the deal you renew with each chess match
As you create issues to pend real issues.

I am the granddaughter of the mixed identities,
Heading to a not-known destination,
Between the horsemen of this chess board.

Our lives are threatened,
By the oily skins you want to lick,
Off our ancestors' lands.

When the CPA arrived,
It was thought a breakthrough,
Weaved by sheets of protocols.

You shocked us with postponements;
Whose is the Referendum of Abyei?
Is it for Mahmmed, Deng, Kuol or Kiir?

The Independence of South Sudan was the hope of my ancestors
Their freedom,
Not to be determined by the oil in their hands.

And now,
We are no more but projects,
Pastoralists coming and going with seasons.

Our security is a nightmare,
We are the returnees,
Who never left.

We no more define peaceful coexistence,
Whether with Warrap or Western Kurdofan,
The Ngok Dinka and the Misseriya Ajaira in Noong,
We live between cultures of lost identities.

Our oily skins are bruised
As we watch the Misseriya graze cattle and eat roasted chicken
As we starve and roam rightless.

 I am granddaughter to Juan Ayak of Abyei
Of that land of bleeding lives so dead
Watching slaughtered dreams, slaughtered lives, looted of future.

But now, I want to clear my tears
I want to unbury my culture and unforget my land.
I want to see Abyei
The land of my ancestors.

# Jenge

*Grace Aben Kuol*

In a family burning with grudges and hatred, should I hold grudges too? Against whom? I ask myself, as I bump into one grumpy face after another.

My name is Aluel. Growing up, I was a chubby little girl from Sudan. Now it is another country. It became South Sudan after the split in 2011. I come from Upper Nile, from a tribe of tall, dark, and slender people, but here I am! A short, chubby, Dinka girl. That might be because I was born to an Equatorian woman. Mum is from the Bari tribe in Equatoria. She has a light complexion, a curvy, beautiful body and full lips like mine. She was short too, as my dad's relatives always remarked, even in her hearing. When we were alone as children, we would call my dad's people arrogant. "Why do they say our mum is too short?" we would ask ourselves and giggle, but we never asked them directly. Between Dad's dark skin, and Mum's light skin, I was brown.

My dad actually was not that tall either. He was about 1.75 meters, which was not considered tall in his tribe. Most of his relatives were very tall. They were as tall as the neem trees in our compound which we would spend days trying to climb and never reaching the top.

Growing up, I lived in Khartoum with Mum and Dad, my junior sister Akur, and my brother Tiop. Tiop was the youngest among us. Like most South Sudanese households, our house was always full of people. We always lived with relatives, mostly from the side of my dad. At any given time in our house, we were fifteen or thereabout. Our home was not big. It was only two bedrooms, two living rooms, a kitchen, two toilets, and two small yards, one at the back and another in front. By God's mercy, that house tolerated us for more than nine years. But that also meant that we got in each other's way and were in each other's faces all the time. When we were up to mischief, we did not have anywhere to hide. But sometimes it was fun having people around all the time.

I remember when Akur was six years old, and I was nine, people said she was a mini copy of me. Back then, people said we had the same wide, dark-brown eyes, the same round face, the same complexion, and the same gap between our upper front teeth so our smiles looked the same too. When my mum's friends would come to visit us, they would look at photographs of me on the wall when I was six years old and they would say, "These pictures of Akur are beautiful." Mum had to explain to visitors that it was me in all those photographs, and not Akur. There were some differences between us, though. She was left-handed, about seven centimetres shorter than me, and she didn't talk much. She was a quiet girl, always by herself especially when there were visitors around. Later when we grew up, we each started getting distinct features and stopped confusing people.

As we were growing up, my brother was the cutest thing I knew in the world. When he was only three years old he could speak Dinka more fluently than Akur and I. He had a very good Dinka vocabulary. None of us could compete with him. I always thought to myself, "This boy is a genius." Of course, he had the advantage of staying home as a toddler, where most of the people spoke Dinka. Akur and I, on the other hand, went to school and started learning English and Arabic. Pupils in school only spoke Arabic, so we had to learn Arabic to communicate, which made us forget some of the words and concepts in our language. Tiop was chubby too, but his lips were smaller. I envied him.

Growing up in that house of two different ethnic groups, I learned that some Dinka and Bari did not like each other. But it was also very confusing because some of them would marry each other out of love, as my dad and mum did.

One morning, I woke up and thanked God I had not wet my bed at night. Tiop and Akur were still sleeping. Waking up in dry beds made us start our day very content. We would feel confident and pleased with ourselves. It was like we had won the battle of our lives. And even though we didn't know what would happen the following day, we lived in the moment and celebrated the start to our day with smiles of hope and happiness. But when we wet our beds, we woke up sad and scared. The room would smell like a goat-house and we hated it. It was always a nightmare. I never wanted to wet my bed. No one respects a nine-year-old girl who still wets her bed.

My cousins used to laugh at me and my mum used to beat me. I would hide the wet bedsheet every time, flip the mattress, put a folded bedsheet at the wet place and then lay a new clean bed sheet, hoping it would dry and go unnoticed so I would not have to go through that torture. But many times the plan failed because of the smell, and they would discover the wet bedsheets and blanket.

I tip-toed out of the room so I wouldn't wake my siblings who were still snoring. I went into the living room and moved to the back yard looking for people and for tea. Indeed, tea was ready. It was served from a red Thermos flask that stood on a dark-brown mahogany table. There was fresh bread too, sprinkled with flour. They had just brought it from the nearby bakery. "It must still be hot, just as I love it," I thought to myself as I approached. It looked delicious on a white plate. It smelled like life to my empty stomach.

My Aunties, Doky and Olivia, were already up and chatting in the backyard. I smiled at them as I approached to take some tea and bread. I then remembered I had not brushed and neither had I washed my face. Hmm, I shook my head but continued. I was not ready to go back. "My mouth does not smell bad. I can brush my teeth later. My face is okay. Mum has not seen me," I told myself, as I looked at the bread and swallowed saliva.

Before I greeted my aunties, they turned to me and started talking, "*Ma yaw harakat ta dinka de*,"[48] Auntie Doky said as she looked at me with disgust. I knew she wasn't mad at me particularly, but I also knew I reminded her of injustice, of hatred, of pain. One could think she was looking at a filthy dog that had stumbled in to her food. I did not answer because I did not quite

48    That is Dinka behaviours

understand what she was talking about. She continued *"Arian Jenge sakit."*[49] "Did she mean me?" I questioned quietly, as I quickly looked at myself up and down, checking my yellow shirt and blue skirt. Why? I am not naked, I said to myself wondering why she was saying I was naked and with so much disgust.

The bread did not smell good anymore and everything in that place shouted at me with rejection.

*"Mallu Kaman Aunti?"*[50] I asked with disappointment and sadness, but hoping to get explanations and maybe reasons behind her insult to me.

*"Ita ma asuma kalam alwonoso fi radio de? Dinka katulo nas fi Kajokeji ombarih bilel,"*[51] she said angrily. But how would I know what had been said on radio? I never used to listen to the radio. Evenings, when everybody else crowded around the radio was our best time to play. That would be the moment we would play with abandon; no one would bother calling us or even checking on us to know where we were or whether we were safe. But of course, I knew some things because I would overhear my father and mother talking.

I frowned with denial for a moment, then I gazed back at my auntie. I would not dare tell her that she was wrong to treat me like that. It was true that some Dinka killed people in Kajokeji, but I did not even know them. It did not make sense to me why she would talk to me with hate because of someone else's crimes. I could not tell her that I wished she could love me like Hanadi's auntie, who hugged Hanadi and cuddled her when she came to see her results at school. I would look at them the whole time. I wished I was her. She was a lucky girl, I always said to myself. She told me many stories about her maternal aunties who loved her so much. She loved them too. But instead my aunties were busy telling me things I did not want to hear. Things I had nothing to do with. I felt unloved.

---

49      Just a naked Dinka (The Dinka refer to themselves as Jieng, but people from Equatoria call them Jenge.)
50      But what is it Auntie?
51      Didn't you hear what they were saying on the radio? The Dinka killed people in Kajokeji last night.

I asked myself, "Who were those Dinka?" Well, whoever they were, they committed crimes. Killing is a sin as Pastor William had said the previous Sunday. But it was not me killing people. I would not do that. I could not even kill the ant that bit my butt the day before. How would I kill a person? No. Not me. I would not deny people's rights. Even right at home, I would not deny anyone's rights. If mummy asked me to distribute biscuits after lunch, I gave Akur and Tiop equal shares and would take two biscuits for myself, just like them. Mum says we are all equal and I must know people's rights and respect them.

I stood still, absent minded. I was lost in my thoughts. My eyes were wide open, but I was not seeing anything. I was overwhelmed by my conflict of identity. It felt like my heart was too heavy to function normally. I was so sad and sorry because some Dinka people were doing bad things. But I loved my dad. He was Dinka too, but he was not killing other people. Those innocent souls being killed matter. Yes, they matter. No one should be robbed of their homes, their safety or their lives in their own country. But should I be blamed for what others did, because they happened to be from my tribe? I did not think so. I turned round and walked away from the back yard and headed back into the house. The house felt smaller than usual. In a moment I bumped into my dad and gasped for air. I looked up and asked him, "Baba, why does Auntie Doky call us *arian jenge sakit*?"

Before my father could respond, I started weeping. He knelt down before me and looked into my eyes. He then held my chubby hands and said in a very soft voice, "My girl, some people from our tribe committed horrendous crimes, and they might not be forgiven for that. But it is not your fault my dear. Lions that think the forest belongs to them alone, will make all the other animals to stand up against them because the forest was made for all, and every animal matters."

"Yes Baba," I said, sniffing.

"Never be so proud like those lions. Care for everyone. Be bold, and face every lion with the truth, because they fear it. Although house cats and lions are from the same family, we cannot kill the house cat for the wrongs of the lion. Instead, we should look for the lion and hunt it down." I was still trying to understand the story of the lion and the other animals when Dad stormed away.

"Your auntie will see. Today she will see what I am made of. How can she dare call my daughter names in my house?" He roared like thunder as he called out my aunt's name. "Doky! Doky!"

Auntie Doky did not answer.

"Where is she?"

"She is there in the backyard." I pointed with one hand at the door leading to the backyard while the other wiped the tears rolling on my face.

When dad opened the door, Auntie Doky was not in the backyard. She must have left when she heard my dad speak to me.

"Where is she?" he asked again. Dad slammed the door behind us as we went back inside.

As I trotted behind my strong and loving dad in search of Auntie Doky, the fire inside me died down. Dad turned and looked at me.

"You see my daughter, we do not have to hold any grudges," he said. We should just be good humans. Will the fight between the lions and the other animals end? Yes, it will. With love, forgiveness, accountability and commitment, it will die down."

"Hmm," I nodded as I breathed the burden of the insults off my chest.

# My papers
*Layet Busena*

My first time being a refugee came by default because I was born in a refugee camp. My parents had run for safety from the Southern Sudan, now South Sudan, due to continuous armed conflict. In 1989, they arrived in Kitgum in Northern Uganda where there was a transit camp, and they later transferred to Agojo refugee settlement in Adjumani. When UNHCR started organizing repatriation in 2016, they did not accept to return. Up to now, my family still lives in the refugee settlement in Uganda.

I repatriated to South Sudan on my own and I moved to Juba, the capital city of the world's youngest nation. It felt like I was in another world, not my own country. Whenever my fellow South Sudanese spoke, it seemed like just meaningless noise, because I could not understand even a mere greeting in Arabic yet it was the language everyone used. Every home at least had a fence either made of bamboo or bricks, and there were numerous tea spots where men would gather the whole day smoking shisha and drinking tea. It was a very different situation from what I was used to in Uganda.

I had spent only fifteen days in Juba when another war broke out at the presidency while the president and his vice were in a meeting together. The fighting started among their guards but then spilled into communities, leading to killings between the Nuer and Dinka tribes and against other tribes of South Sudan. There was killing, but also looting, and destroying property such as houses and vehicles. That is when I ran away by myself. I had never experienced such massive killing and destruction. I did not believe my eyes, seeing armed men, well dressed in proper army uniforms, who were supposed to protect citizens, turn round and kill them. My uncle was shot dead on the spot right in front of me. At first, I thought he had just knocked his toe on a stone and fallen, because I never saw the bullet come. But then I saw blood and I saw him lie lifeless. I turned away from him and continued running without knowing where I was heading. I found myself at a border point on the road in the morning.

I am now 24 years, a trained primary school teacher. I want to return to my country to serve my people by teaching but also to participate in creating change. Many people in South Sudan have not yet appreciated education, and many have not had the chance to go to school due to the continuous wars that have forced people to live in bushes and in exile, where all they think about is survival. For most South Sudanese, staying in school and studying is not an option. Sometimes some people go to refugee camp schools, but those schools do not offer strong education and in the end, there is a high rate of school dropouts.

I remember when I was in primary school, my best friend and classmate called Adul dropped out of school. Before that, she had been injured with bullets on both thighs during the Garang war, while she was running to Uganda. She and others running fell into an ambush of soldiers around Lobone, in Eastern Equatoria state. Till her death, she would remember the sound of her bones as they were being shattered by bullets and how she immediately became paralyzed. She bled unconscious and was later picked with other causalities by the government soldiers after the ambush was cleared. They transported them to Juba hospital. She described sleeping among dead bodies in the ward for many days since she could not move her body but just lay still on her back. After several surgeries, she at least was able to walk again but because she never really received proper treatment. At the start, her limbs could hardly touch the ground, even after she was healed. To take one step would take her about a minute of negotiations with her body. She was as slow as a chameleon. In a week, she would attend classes a maximum of three days. She would complain that the scars hurt especially on cold morning when she would have to wake up early and start walking to school. During exams, Adul would write for just about the first 15 minutes and then fall asleep. Every end of term, when we received our report cards, she would be among the last five pupils who the teachers would call out to the front of the whole school. This humiliated and discouraged her and in the end, she dropped out of school. While the teachers probably did it for fun, it had an extreme negative effect on the children.

It is such cases that made me decide to go back to South Sudan, to be part of the education system and teach South Sudanese children. I left Uganda in December 2016. I only carried a few personal things like clothing, academic papers, and my refugee identity documents. I left all my family members behind. I went back on my own, without assistance from the government or from UNHCR. I did not even inform the Ugandan Office of the Prime Minister (OPM), which managed Kiryandongo refugee settlement, where I lived. I travelled alone without any friend or family member.

When the bus reached the Nimule border point at around 5am, the immigration officers ordered all of us to come out of the bus. One officer asked me to prove that I was South Sudanese, by showing my travel documents and identity card. I showed them the refugee identity card. He looked at me in a strange way and took the card to the boss. He said nothing so I thought I would just receive a clearance from the boss. Instead, the boss came to where I stood, sweeping his way through the other passengers like the monsoon winds. He came with five bodyguards. They all wanted to see the refugee travelling to Juba. The officer looked me up and down, probably studying my petit size and comparing me to residents of Juba. He looked at me and said, "*Ya biniya, bed takum wen? Iti min yatu gebila?*"[52]

I had no idea what he was talking about since I neither speak nor understand Arabic. I kept looking at his officers and expecting them to give him a reply. I thought he was probably giving them some instructions. I remained quiet as he continued talking. I could only hear noises, which had no meaning to me. At some point, his eyes changed and looked like those of lion about to

52      Young girl, where is your home? What tribe are you from?

pounce on its prey. I began to suspect that he was probably feeling disrespected by my silence. He said something which sounded like a final command, then four well-dressed men in black suits walked over to me and led me away. They pulled me along, my feet hardly touching the ground. Apparently, the officer just had ordered my arrest and detention. As they took me to the cell, they explained to me that all along the officer had been asking me in Arabic to say where my home was and which tribe I was from.

When I got inside the cell, I was amused that a cell could be a permanent building because I had never slept in one before. I was used to the small thatched huts in the refugee settlement where I had lived since childhood. The detention cell was a dark room. Being inside there was like being outside in the night during those seasons when there is no moon in the sky. I could hardly tell whether it was day or night. The cell had no windows, but it had a wooden door with ventilation slits close to the roof. But there was cloth tied across the slits, blocking out air and light.

I stayed in that room for three days without any food and without anyone to speak to. It was the last supper of beans and the yellow posho distributed by World Food Programme that I had with my *Abuba*[53] in Kiryandongo that sustained me. I prayed to God all the time. My memory became my companion, because I was able to remember almost all the Sunday school songs that we used to sing as children in my church and kindergarten. I remember I sang about 63 songs. Several times I urinated on myself while seated down just like a baby because there were no buckets, and no prison guards to take me out. The cells smelled like a loafing shed for he-goats or a broken sewage pipe, and I did not care whether the stench was coming from me or from the waste on the cell floor. I had lost all hope. In three days, my weight dropped by over nine kilograms. I became so light that wind could easily sweep me off my feet. . All my belongings— my cell phone and handbag—had been taken away from me by the men who led me to the cell. My other luggage had remained on the bus that left me, stuck in the

53      Grandmother

clearance process at Nimule border checkpoint. It had not occurred to me as I set off from the refugee camp, that I needed papers to prove my nationality, to prove my home. I had always thought that one needs papers to leave home, but not to return.

After three days in the cell, at around 10am, I heard someone call my name, Layet! Layet! Layet! I first kept quiet. I knew that could easily signal the end for me. I crawled and slouched in one of the corners of the cell. Within no time, the door cracked open. A very bright torchlight flooded the room. I quietly said, "I am here," sounding like a two-year-old child. Maybe my vulnerability led to a change of heart, because at that point his voice became calm. He said to me, "Come here, young girl. We are going to the boss. He wants to see you." I do not know where I got the energy from, but I stood up and started walking towards him. I was feeling so weak from hunger and isolation. As I walked towards him, the weakness overpowered me again, and I fell to the floor. He ran into the cell, held my hand and raised me up. Slowly, we walked to his boss who was stationed about one km away from the cells. It took us almost two hours to arrive where he was because I was too weak. When we got to him, he asked me for two hundred US dollars so that he could help and release me. I told him, "Sir please, I am coming from a refugee camp. I don't have that amount of money." And I was thinking that even my father has never held such money. I started weeping.

As I still stood in front of the boss wondering what my fate was going to be, another man walked in. He was speaking Kiswahili and he said he was from Kenya. He started talking to me. He said, "Young girl, what is the problem? Have you lost someone?" I said, "No sir." "Then why are you crying?" he continued. I had no words to say to him, so I kept quiet. The man who had just brought me from the cell narrated my ordeal to him. The man comforted me and asked the boss to allow him pay fifty dollars on my behalf. The boss laughed and accepted. He said," It is only because you are my friend that I accept your offer." I was joyful but when I smiled, my dry lips cracked. I had not realised how dehydrated I had become in the three days. The man paid the fifty dollars and also purchased a temporarily travel document for me. He held my hand and supported me out of the man's office. This kind man took me with him up to Juba.

When I reached Juba, I was very excited to see the land where I belong. But it was also a sad moment to be in a land that has swallowed a lot of landmines and bombs. Along the Nimule-Juba highway, we had encountered many warning roadside signs painted either red or red and white. These went on until the Juba Bridge, after Sherikat. Sometimes the warnings were also painted on stones and trees. The man who was still with me took me to the bus office to check for my luggage, but we did not find even one piece. We left the bus station and the man took me to a supermarket. I cannot even explain how I smelt. I had worn same knicker, t-shirt, and trouser, for four days. I felt humiliated but there was nothing I could do. Even the air refresher and air conditioner in the man's car could not subdue the smell. The man kept on sneezing and I knew it was because of the odour from my body and clothes. At the supermarket, he bought for me a knicker, a bra, and some personal hygiene items. The challenge now was how to connect with the friends and relatives in Juba as my only cell phone had been taken away from me at the detention point at Nimule border. The man drove me to his home. As soon as we got home, he showed me to the bathroom, and I took a bath. I don't know how long I stayed in there, but I scrubbed my skin until it ached. I wanted to remove not only the dirt but all traces of the cell too. I changed into the new clothes he had bought for me. Shortly after we settled in, he took me to look for food at a nearby restaurant. When he asked me how much I would eat, I said I would eat two plates. He laughed and bought the food but before I finished one plate, my stomach could not stretch any more. I carried the second plate home. The three days of extreme hunger in the dark cells had shrunk my stomach. We returned home after the food and slept.

In the morning when we woke up, we started talking. I learnt that Kamau was working with Care International as a Livelihoods Officer based in Juba. I spoke to him about my interest in working in my home-country, South Sudan. I told him that my first priority was to attain a national identity card and passport in order to ease my stay and travels. My family was still in the refugee camp in Uganda. Mr. Kamau promised to help. He also offered me his cell-phone and I spoke to Baba. I knew his telephone number off head. Baba listened as I narrated my border experience. We both cried. Kamau who was looking on also cried. Baba spoke to Kamau and thanked him for being good-hearted and asked for God's blessing upon him. Kamau promised to take good care of me as I settled in.

This was now my new home. Kamau gave me money for lunch and emergency upkeep before he left for work. I remained home doing laundry and resting since I had spent three stressful days in the cells. I was only worried about how I could acquire a national identity card and passport of my country since my temporary travel document was only valid for three months. In the evening, I was home when he returned. "Layet," he called me. "I have this for you," he said handing me an envelope. I looked inside, and it was a cell-phone. "Now you can communicate with your family as regularly as you want." I felt delighted at the opportunity to speak with my people as often as I wanted. I told Kamau how grateful I was and I prayed to God to bless him abundantly for all he had done for me. He was the most warm-hearted person I had ever met. He became my only relative at that point.

The following morning, he dropped me off at the Ministry of Internal Affairs to start with the process of acquiring an ID and passport.

Kamau brought me more clothes each time he returned from work. We always had supper together at a restaurant and he always provided me money for lunch and upkeep for all the days I was in Juba. It felt comfortable and I began to plan my future in

Juba. I was getting used to the way of life and I was sure I would cope with it.

A few days later, one Monday morning at around 6am, Kamau woke me up. "Let us prepare very fast and go to follow-up with your documents. My friend told me that people who are processing their documents from that office always sleep around the compound to pick the forms for registration." I quickly brushed my teeth and got dressed without bathing. I did not want to delay him. I never wanted to annoy him at all. As soon as I was ready, we jumped into his car and he drove at a speed of 120km per hour to Juba's main hospital to first acquire an age assessment or birth certificate. I got the certificate but that was after spending almost eleven hours at the hospital even though we had the help of Kamau's friend who was a doctor there. Kamau picked me and we passed by the restaurant to eat our supper. I told him how the day had gone and how everything was difficult. We agreed that the following day we should leave home even earlier.

We left home by 5:30am. He made a call to one of his friends, Mr. Offere, and asked him to help me during the process since I could not speak even one word in Juba Arabic. The friend came and we started the journey of documents.

Starting right at the gate, every person was speaking in Arabic. How could I not speak a single word of the language my people spoke? I was enraged. I felt like I was in another country. I felt like a refugee again.

Kamau's friend stayed by my side. He walked with me to the first office to pick the forms. As soon as we entered, the officer at the desk spoke to me in Arabic, "*Jinsia,*"[54] he said. I did not understand, so I just stared at him, hoping he would explain in English. Before I could explain my situation, the officer, barking like a dog, started to chase us out of his office. The man I was with tried to interpret, "He wants to know your nationality. Show your identity card." "Which South Sudanese can't speak Arabic! Move

---

54    National Identity Card

out of my office and give way to citizens," he shouted. I turned to ask Kamau's friend to translate but he had already flown from the barking man, abandoning me in there. Desperate, I stayed, begging.

After a short while I saw him return but he did not enter the office. He stood at the door-way and signalled for me to come out. I had not yet got the papers when he summoned me but I moved out to check what it was he wanted. He told me that there was fighting taking place and that we had to leave immediately. I moved away with him and never went back for my papers.

I ran back to the refugee camp where I still live today. My home is now the refugee camp. I am grateful to those who developed the non-refoulement policy that prohibits a refugee from being forced to return to his/her country. In my case though, I do not fear repatriation, but I do not have a home to return to even when peace returns to South Sudan. It seems I don't belong there.

I do not know.

# I Wanted to belong to no one

*Kiden Jackline*

A lot happened. We had to leave the place we called home. The place of so many memories. A place we thought we would live our entire lives. Something bad came up that made us leave. We had to go and look for a place where we could find refuge. That was some years back.

Leaving our family in that way was not easy. How do you step over your blood and walk without looking back? How do you leave without paying your last respects? But my mother grabbed me in my night wear, and we started moving through the villages.

"We must walk until we reach Moyo," she said to me. "Moyo is the safest place close to Kajokeji."

Quietly, I trotted next to her.

But Moyo was not near. More people joined us as we fled. We had to spend the night on the way, and we spent it in water. My mother said it was safer to stay in water with our heads submerged as much as possible so that those chasing us would not see us and kill us. We could hear the gunshots in the villages. There were a lot of people in the stream. Up to today I wonder how we managed to spend a night in water. Who sleeps in water? Some men grabbed leafy branches and covered the parts of the stream where people were hiding. At some point, you could see people coming up, because they could not really breathe in water and under leaves. I saw people struggling to survive.

In the morning, we came out of the water and continued our run. On the way we passed a home where we found a woman who told us she had four girls. She was around 68 years or thereabout. She said that soldiers had entered her house and they raped the girls. They forced her to stand by the tree where we found her. We left her and ran on till we reached Moyo in Uganda.

While in Moyo, my mother connected with her elder sister in Kampala and she sent us money for transport. We took a bus, and then a ferry because we had to cross over to Adjumani from

Moyo. When we were on the ferry and I saw how the water was moving with force, I remembered how we were forced to spend a night in the stream when leaving Kajokeji. Although my mother had tried to explain, I still could not understand why we had to sleep in water, and why those men had to put big leaves to cover us like we were not human beings. The whole experience flooded back to memory. That made crossing the River Nile quite hard. My mother sat close to me and comforted me. She and other people on the ferry did not know why I kept shaking. Then we crossed to Adjumani safely and continued to Kampala. My mother's sister came for us at the bus park and we went to her house where she lived with her husband and children. She welcomed us but only on the first day. By the second day, it felt like we were invading her privacy. My mother was working so hard to impress my aunt so she could keep us longer in her house. That was our first place of refuge in Kampala. My other sisters were also in Kampala, but they were in school studying. They had been in Kampala for a while.

The house had three rooms, a store and a small compound. My mother and I used to sleep in the store, which was close to the kitchen. There was one bed which we shared. Every morning we would wake up and prepare breakfast. Our hosts would go to work while their children went to school. We would cook lunch and clean up the house. One day I asked my mother why I did not join the children to go to school. She told me that we had just fled from Kajokeji, and her sister had not yet thought of finding a school for me.

A few days later my mother asked my aunt if there was a nearby school that I could join. My aunt replied, "I have given you a home to stay in and now you are asking me to take your daughter to school as well?"

"It will just be for a short while until her sisters complete school and start helping out," she said.

"If you want to stay in this house, you and your daughter have to focus on helping out with the house chores in order to make it easy for all of us," she responded.

I heard everything they said to each other because I was in the kitchen. Mother had taken them breakfast in the dining room. Now I knew the reason I was not going to school. We did not have any money to take me to school. We had fled Kajokeji with nothing.

I was puzzled by my aunt's responses to my mother. Yet the two sisters follow each other. People normally say that children who follow each other have an unbreakable bond. After the conversation, mother came to the kitchen crying.

"What is the problem mother?" I asked her. She did not say anything to me. She just held me and cried.

There is a time when one of my cousins fell sick. My mother went with her and aunt to the hospital. When they returned, the child had a cannula for more medication. I looked at the child in amazement because this was all new to me. In Kajokeji, they would just give you injections on the buttocks. So it was my first time to see a cannula. My cousin seemed to be happy about it too. Some weeks later, I fell sick too and mother did not take me to the hospital. I told her that other parents take their children to hospital and the children return with cannulas. She just ignored me.

We stayed at my aunt's house for some time until we realised we had to leave. Something was not right because there were quarrels after quarrels. Insignificant issues would make my aunt and my mother start quarrelling. But maybe we had overstayed our welcome so to say. "We are eating too much food in this house," she would say. It was becoming tough for all of us.

My mother eventually contacted the person who was taking care of my sister to see whether we could get some support. My sister had some savings from the money she was receiving. She paid three months' rent in a small house and also bought for us some beans and maize flour for food to start with. We were happy to finally be on our own. Mother told my aunt that we were moving out.

"We are very grateful for the time we have spent with you in your home. I want to go now and try to start a business and be able to send the girl to school," my mother said

"Perfect. That is what I have been waiting for," my aunt responded.

We did not have even a cent when we were leaving. We even walked from aunt's home to find my sister at Nsambya. And it is not a short distance. We were so tired by the time we found her. My feet were hurting, but I was happy to see her and reconnect with her. We had not seen each other in many years. It was a happy moment for the family. She took us to our new home - a one-room house in Nsambya, Kevina. In the beginning, it was not easy. My sister always gave us some money from her small allowance. She was at university and needed some pocket-money while we were at home and needed something to eat. Sharing her little money was an indication that we were just in the struggle together as a family.

A couple of times, we ate once in a day. Sometimes there would even be no food and mother would fry some tomatoes and onions as sauce. She made it in a nice way. Right now, I would not eat it perhaps, but back then, I enjoyed it served with posho. At some point that was all we would eat for the day. Then she would tell me, "Drink a lot of water. That is the only way you will grow tall and strong." When I thought about it later, I knew she would tell me that because we did not have enough food to eat. So whenever we cooked that little sauce, she would always say, "Take a lot of water. Eat big posho, even if the sauce is small, eat big posho and take a lot of water!" In our pains, there was a bit of fun.

That is how we started living by ourselves, independently. My sister got some money and gave it to my mother to start a business. Mother bought groundnuts and started selling them at the roadside. She would not go far away like to town. She would just sell from within and around Nsambya. She would go every morning and return around 5pm. She would call me to sit with her and we would count the coins from the day's sale. We would then drop some of the coins in a small container where she used to keep her savings. I enjoyed those moments.

Mother's business started growing. Our situation too started to improve. We started having two meals a day and breakfast with an accompaniment. Before that, there was nothing like breakfast accompaniment because money was always scarce. She started her business selling 2 kilos of groundnuts a day. By evening, they would all be sold out. She saw that she could actually sell even more. She added on one kilo to make three kilos. She went on to make hard-corns too. Her hard-corns were crunchy. She would first boil them, dry them in the sun, and then fry them in oil till they looked golden. She would then drain them and add salt.

The business kept growing, and she kept adding the kilos. I remember there was a time when she would make 10 kilograms to sell it all in a day. That was really good because she was able to save some money and at the same time feed us. She also started paying the rent. At that time, the house was 100,000 UGx. It was one room with the kitchen and a toilet. She started looking after herself and even gave my sister an allowance to do her own things.

Later, mother called my sister Lydia to come and live with us. Lydia was in high-school by then. After a short while all my sisters joined us and we were all living together. Joyce was in university. Annette had dropped out of school and got married. She already had a baby boy, Eddy, who was two years old at the time. She came to the house with him.

We used to get visitors. My mother is very welcoming, so although we were staying in one room, people used to come to visit and would sleep over. Life was difficult, but they could not see that. They would just come. They would not even call. They just came. And she would welcome them. Sometimes we would wonder how she would feed them. But she would just pick from her small savings and buy food. Some people would stay for a week. It was so bad. Most of the time when they would come, we would give up our beds and squeeze ourselves in small spaces to sleep. Mother always wanted visitors to sleep comfortably. She would completely forget about her children when there would be visitors. That was something.

There was a time when I used to fall sick very often, but mother would never take me to the hospital. After every one or two weeks, I would be down with a fever or flu. I kept wondering why she could not take me to the hospital, but given the conditions we were in at that time, there was nothing like going to the hospital or seeing a doctor. I did not understand at the time that my mother was struggling to give us a comfortable life. Later when I was much older, I realised that mother too never went to the hospital. Because she was working really hard, she eventually developed a back problem, but she kept working. She too could not see any doctor. We would just massage her back with pain balm. She used to say that my hands were very hard. Whenever I massaged her. I would do it with the intention of making the pain stop. I would massage her with a lot of energy. She would say, "I do not want Kiden's hands." But I would still massage her. I could insist because I did not want to see her in pain. She was aging and she was continuing to work. It was exhausting for her.

My mother had this medicine that she got from a friend. The medicine looked like a black stone. If you touched it, you would feel like you were touching sugar mixed with a little water. I always looked for it in the house because I wanted to throw it away. It was the only medication we had in the house. She would give it to me when I would had a flu or a fever. If anything happened to me that was health-related, she would just go inside the house and return with the stone. She would take a knife and scrape until a piece dropped off. She would drop the piece in hot water in a small cup and wait for it to melt. The water would then turn black. She would then give it to me to drink. Her medicine was horrible. And you know what she would do? She would make me sit right next to her and ask me to take it all. She would not let me take it from somewhere else where she would not be looking at me. And I think she did not know the dosage because it was generally always one cup, for all of us and for all ailments!

One time I had a fever that made me really shake a lot. I was scared. I told mother, "I'm not feeling well, I really need to go to the hospital."

"I do not have money to take you to the hospital. There is a lot I have to do, so it is ok if you can take that medicine," she told me.

"I really can't take that medicine again," I told her.

"You know your father died," she told me, and narrated to me the story of my father and how he died when I was two years and how she was later forced out of her marital home by in-laws.

Still, I was determined not to take the medicine again. Whenever I took it, I do not even know how to explain how it felt. Incidentally, it would somehow clear all the signs of any sickness. I would take it, and then she would send me to sleep and cover me up with a blanket. I hate having my head covered. I always want my head to be out. But she would cover me fully with a thick blanket. By the time she would uncover me, I would be all-sweaty. Interestingly, I would feel renewed. I would not be sick anymore which was nice. The challenge was in taking the medicine. When I would be taking it, I would feel terrible. I would feel like I should not be taking it. Like it is just not right. But then I would have to take it because that was the only medication we could access as a family.

When I saw that I could not convince mother to change her mind and take me to the hospital, I decided I would not argue with her again because I felt like she did not really love me. I did not see others taking a lot of that medicine. It looked like it was mainly meant for me. In my young mind it felt like she wanted to kill me or do something strange to me. But again, it was me falling sick most of the time and as a result, I took it more than my siblings.

I do not know how to describe that medication. I would look at it and think, someone wants to kill me. But then again, when I would take it and feel better, I would have second thoughts. But honestly, whenever I looked at that medicine, I thought, someone intends to kill me. Someone wants me dead. I would think about all of the negative things.

So, one evening, I just decided to leave home. I left the house for two reasons: because I thought my mother wanted to kill me and because I thought I was becoming a burden in the house due to being the sickly child. So those were the two things that drove me out of home. I felt that going out there, without anyone to take care of me, I would just face life the way it came. If anything bad happened, then people would just forget about me. That is what came to my mind.

So I left the house.

I was on the street for one week. Believe me, it was the first experience of being homeless in my life. Not even in Kajokeji after we were kicked out of my father's house was I homeless. Being on the street taught me what it meant to be homeless, and I realised I had never been homeless. On the first night on the street, I slept on the veranda of a shop after looking for something to eat from a pile of garbage. I was very hungry. I had not eaten anything that day. I did not have any money, not even a coin, nothing. I had left home with one dress which was sowed from a cloth which had belonged to my grandmother. She used it as a wrapper. My mother had told me, "This wrapper belonged to your grandmother and she gave it to me." She usually has this way of saying, "Kiden, have this. It belonged to my mother." She respects the practise of inheriting things. It is not a practise in South Sudan, to pass on something from a grandmother to a granddaughter. They will only pass on the name. They do not pass on clothes, or earrings, or bracelets. They will not do that. Instead they look at who she loved the most and then they give the things to that person. But they will not say, oh your grandmother left this for you. OR your grandmother used to love this so much, you can have it. No.

I took with me that dress from the wrapper when I left home. I actually did not have much in terms of clothes. We all did not have much. Remember, I ran from Kajokeji in a nightdress. So mother went and sewed that wrapper into a dress for me when we got to Kampala. That was the only thing that was sentimental to me. I still have that dress. Sometimes, when I'm telling the story of our journey, I wear that dress. Sometimes I just get it, put it on, wash it, iron it and put it back. That is the dress I escaped in. It is the only dress that gave me comfort and that I felt belonged to me.

Look at my life transforming. From Kajokeji, to my aunt's house, to the street and now to an independent graduate woman.

When I looked at the life of, you cannot go to the hospital, you can't go to school, we don't have money, we have to eat posho tomatoes and onions, we have to eat only once a day, breakfast can't have an accompaniment and so on, I felt like there was no point to living in a family. I thought, "Just live on the streets and maybe one day, hunger will just strike you and you will die. Nobody will bother asking how you disappeared."

One week on the street was unbearable. I got rained on. I tried to take shelter on someone's veranda but they chased me away. I went to another veranda and found there some street children. At least I got some company, though it was people I did not know. They were Karamajongs. I started interacting with them. When I look back, I think God was with me because anything could have happened. They could have raped me and the other small girls. We were basically sleeping on the streets. We would just find a space and then sleep.

Sometimes we had nothing at all to eat and we would just stay hungry. I did not beg although I was in need. I would just look in trash cans or sit near people who would be eating. If they felt sympathetic, they would give me something.

One day, I just decided to walk through Nsambya. My base was locally known as Detawo, in Katwe, just near the rail line. That is where I would go and sleep with other homeless children. I just thought of taking a walk towards where our house was. By that time, my mother was living in a two roomed house, which was within walking distance from my base. So I took the walk. This time, I was hoping I could get someone who knew me, because I was tired of living on the street. I was tired of being homeless. I was tired of living a life without reason. We would just wake up to nothing. I did not shower for the whole week.

As I walked, I heard someone say, "Oh my god, is that you Kiden?" I turned to look at who it was. She was a friend of my mother. She said, "Your mother has been looking for you."

She told me that my mother was sick and that she had been looking for me, up to the point that she could not talk. She was bedridden. I was touched that I did not know what was happening to my family after I left. I did not even think it would hurt them, because I thought I was just an inconvenience. I did not think that my disappearance would hurt my mother to the extent of making her sick. That was really mind-blowing. Of course I did not want anything to happen to my mother. I just wanted her to be fine. I thought the only way for her to be fine was for me to disappear so she would not have the troubles of my medication, or of finding money for my school fees. I just wanted to be on the streets and belong to no one. I did not know it would badly affect mother.

My mother's friend asked me if she could take me home.

"Yes, I would like to see my mother," I said.

"Come," she said. She was very kind to me and I knew that she loved my mother.

When we got home, we found people seated with Mother, telling her that I would be found, because I did not know Kampala well enough to go far. Surprisingly, they expected me anytime soon. I remained behind the door while the woman who had taken me went inside the house. I heard her speak to my mother.

"There is someone here to see you," she said.

"Let the person come in," my mother responded.

The woman called me into the house. She did not do it like, Kiden is here! No. This helped because I was just feeling ashamed for putting my mother in such a situation. The woman held my hand and brought me close. When my mother saw me, oh my God!

She was lying down. She got up from the bed and I saw tears in her eyes, like she was thinking, finally my girl is here! I could clearly see that she was happy to see me. Despite my not bathing for a week, she hugged me as she cried. I could clearly see that she had missed me.

She did not ask me about why I left. She just embraced me. We took time hugging despite my bad smell, I had not bathed for a week. But she kept cuddling me in her arms. And that really felt very nice. In the normal African way, a child who runs away from home and is discovered, first gets caned before anything else. But my mother embraced me and all the friends who had come to see her told her that it was a good moment. They told her that she was a good mother. I think I had missed that hug too. It was really a good one. Maybe I should get lost again. But now she is old, and I am no longer a child.

The Peace We Yearn For

# Differences Alike

*Lucy Kiden Lulu*

Once we own up to our imperfect human nature,
Acknowledge the likenesses in our differences
That each compliments the other
Then we can coexist in this diverse nation we call home.

The peace we yearn for,
The calm we call for
It's already there, lingering
Let's embrace it all, these pieces of us!
And if we can defend each other,
Then we deserve each other.

# Are You Warm?

*Nyankiir Nyandeng Chaat*

Who are you?

What are you?
Are you real?
How do you feel?
Are you warm?
Are you cool?
In the bushes, my grandfathers and their ancestors searched for you.
They dispelled their pain in the squeezed triggers.
Many have died for you, you know?
Our grandmothers, mothers, aunts, sisters, left home to look for you.
Is it not time to come out of hiding?
Let us feel you,
Let us love you
Allow us to savour your body and tap your honey, like a woman's sanctuary
This time, we will tighten our grip and hold on to your sap,

We promise we won't bite.

# Here

*Lydia Minagano Kape*

Here
I am shattered
But every shred feels whole
Here
I find bliss for my soul.

Here
My name embodies
Gleam, like that of the stars
Here
The Nile sings for me
The birds wake me up.

Here
We sing to the moon
The sky baptizes us.

Here
I indulge
To the warmth of the sun
Here, my feet kiss
The melanin soil.

Here
The soil where my offspring
Shall entrench their roots
Here
They shall blossom fruits.

Here
My roots are found
Here I belong
Here is home.

# Unity is Strength
*Hellena Rial Isaac Nyariel*

Without unity we will be like a house without pole
We will be like a dog with no tail
We shall live like a sea without water
We will taste like a broth without salt

Unity is strength without which we are like a house without poles
A house without roof
A tree that does not bear fruits
We are mobile phone without a battery

Unity is a rescuer of one's soul
It makes people germinate like crops
Unity decorates rooms of the heart
Makes them shine like the morning sun


# Future's Will
*Hellena Rial Isaac Nyariel*

One day
We shall wake them up
This world which has slept on,
One day
We shall use our candles to light the world,
When the sun stops shining,
One day
We shall bring people together again
When hatred has chased away peace and unity.

We, the children of today,
Hold dreams for the future
As we steadily travel the road to change

# If You are threatened
*Nyareeta Gach*

If you are threatened by a fist: a symbolic gesture of a tradition of withholding retaliation, a mark of resilience, unspoken peace, the strength and unity of the people, then, allow me free one finger.

# Quench the Thirst
*Lucy Kiden Lulu*

Like Raindrops, we are...
Seemingly inconsequential in this big world
But together, we can cause a storm in the desert
A storm to cleanse hearts and minds, refresh souls and grow peace

Like Raindrops, we are different
We are fractions, each bearing a perfect ingredient
We each possess little bits of peace
Puzzle pieces for the Future of South Sudan

Like Raindrops, we fall in separate locations,
Let us soak our paths with
Love, kindness and selflessness
Make it contagious to our surroundings, the people

Like Raindrops we must work together
To quench thirst for peace, and together flow in freedom,
Let us create a river of hope that flows in abundance
In and out of seasons, for the growth of this nation

Like Raindrops, our strength is in unity.

# Fix Me

*Lucy Kiden Lulu*

My heart is broken
Can you fix me?
I am hurting inside
The pain I feel is wearing me out
I am tired of the bloodshed
I am so worn out

What are you doing about it?
What are you saying about it?
What are you thinking about
This pain I feel inside?

Why don't you
Fix me? All I need is love
Fix me. All I need is peace
Fix me. All I need is you to come together
And work together to fix me
I am South Sudan

I am tired of all the hate in the air
I wince at every rumour of revenge
Innocent dying, widows multiplying?
I look around and it's just too much

Junubin, I am yours and you are mine
Each one of you is a puzzle piece
Of this great picture called South Sudan
You are all different
Each difference is an addition
To the growth of this nation

So why don't you fix me?
All I need is Love
All I need is peace
All I need is you to come together
And work together to fix me
I am South Sudan

# Just a single drop

*Susan Thomas Perembata*

Motherland,
Soaked in pools of agony,
Laments of anguish and pain,
Who will save your children?

See how full of tears we are
How sorrows and gunshots surround us
How flames engulf us till all is down to ashes?
Leaving your children life-sentenced to exile.

Motherland,
To live as a refugee is to sign away your life.
With beastly defilers and killers
They rape, they kill.

Motherland,
Where beautiful memories are under siege
No one dares to care,
And no life is spared

Dearest Motherland
Your own children rebel against you,
On our knees we seek peace
Even just a single drop.

# My country
*Hellena Rial Isaac Nyariel*

I was in love with you, my country
But you took away our happiness
And destroyed us.
Brothers and sisters,
Fathers and mothers.
You demolished us.
See,
We are in disarray.
We no longer know who you are.
We have lived in war for decades.
We have been made slaves, treated like pigs.
We keep slaughtering each other in useless pursuits.
Scattered all over the world
When shall we stop this and start to live
Even in ripped pieces
In peace?

# Anew
*Apeay Ogeli*

a stream of consciousness at the highest alkalinity
paranoia embedded between thoughts
soaring through the valley
as the source connects me to the highest consciousness
to find the piece of peace deeper than the sea
giving and giving
to the wrong things
exuberantly filling the souls of many
collapsing underneath the weight of validation
breaking free from the power of others
healing from the pain of the past
making and breaking day by day
to grow anew

# A new beginning

*Susan Thomas Perembata*

9 January 2005 was a special day. It was the day we had all been waiting for. I woke up very early in the morning at about 5.30 am. I was with my sister Teresa. We bathed and put on our best perfumes. Theresa said we needed to start the morning smelling good because we were going to dance and sweat all day. We laughed and hugged and laughed again. We both put on white T-shirts, the costume that everybody had agreed to. We were among the 100 Azande traditional dancers. For the past week, we had been practicing dances to celebrate the signing of the Comprehensive Peace Agreement CPA.

The celebrations were held in Nyayo Stadium. All the Southern Sudanese communities in Nairobi were involved. My friend Nakene and I led our group with songs and dances. We went by bus to the venue and we all lined up outside the stadium. All the dancers were dressed in white T-shirts and white *gaka*.[55] We began dancing even before we got inside the stadium. Excitement filled the air as women swayed from side to side. We sang songs of freedom and kept repeating one particular song which was our favourite: *zereda imayee furani aremeoo*, peace has come for us today.

Nakene was ahead of me and I followed closely. She would start a song, then we would all join in, singing, ululating and whistling. We had drums too. It did not matter that we were not on home ground. We had the *anzoro, akpanigbo and ngbinga* – all traditional Azande percussion instruments. It was only 8am, but we were already sweating wet, our shirts sticking to our bodies. The perfume we had used before leaving home had long evaporated, leaving us to smell like he-goats. But nobody cared. We had our freedom. Most people stayed and danced throughout the day.

---

55    Gaka is the Azande Dance traditional wear

We danced traditional dances from the Dinka, Nuer, Acholi, Bari and many other tribes. Whoever brought a dance into the arena, it was received, and we all joined in. I felt unity among us. Even when we stepped on each other as we danced, it did not matter. Hundreds of people from all over the world came to Nairobi to celebrate and witness the signing of the Peace Agreement. I did not know that one could be full on an empty stomach. We only took water, soda and sweets the whole day, but we did not feel hungry. I guess we were just full of the happiness. The weather too had mercy on us that day. The sun was bright throughout the day, and there was no rain, so we continued the celebration until 6pm in the evening when the stadium closed.

On the bus back home, we continued singing, dancing, clapping our hands and ululating until each person reached his or her final destination. That evening we discussed new jobs in Juba, setting up big businesses selling water and soda, clothes and shoes, running restaurants and opening up supermarkets. We ate chicken, *nyama choma*[56] and fish. We drank soda, beer and Johnnie Walker. We played new songs of peace by Emmanuel Kembe, a popular South Sudanese musician. When we finally went to bed at about 2am, we were exhausted but content.

One week after the celebrations, I travelled to Juba. I had been offered a job in the new government, and I also dreamed of setting up my own business. I was thinking about a supermarket or boutique for both women's and men's wear. I left my daughter Hellen with my brother and his wife. My friend Nakene also remained in Nairobi. I was so excited to board the Eagle Air flight to go back home. We boarded from Wilson Airport in Langata, Nairobi. I travelled with a number of people who had played key roles in the struggle for peace for Southern Sudan: Dr. Mark Zandabeyo, Martin Okello and Grace Datiro. These were prominent politicians who had been living in Nairobi, working for the struggle, and waiting for the peace agreement to be signed so they could go back to take up positions in the Government. Zandabeyo became

56      Grilled meat.

the Deputy Minister of Labour and Public Service, while Grace Datiro became the State Minister for Education. Martin became the Minister of Physical Infrastructure at the National Government.

The plane was small and it made a lot of noise in the air. It also moved very slowly, as if it was too heavy. It felt like it was struggling to climb over the mountains. I was scared but I kept praying to God to enable me, and all the other passengers on the plane, to arrive safely in Juba. It took us about one and a half hours to arrive at Juba International Airport. I was very excited to be back in my country after 14 years in exile. I was so proud. I felt like a child, smiling smiles that I did not need to explain. I had been lost with no identity. I had grown up on my own in exile without any idea of parental love save for some friends who I stayed with. But I was home.

Sadly, I did not see anyone I knew at the airport and nobody came to meet me. My father and my siblings did not know of my coming to Juba because I had not communicated to them. My home is in the village of Madoro in Ezo County, bordering Congo and Central African Republic. It is quite far from Juba, the capital city of South Sudan. My mother had died in 1996 when I was in Uganda. Somehow I got the news but I couldn't go to her funeral and I had never seen her grave. The fact that there was no one to meet me at the airport did not dampen my spirits. After all, I was sure I was going to see my family in a few days. And most important, I was finally going to see my mother's grave.

I was lucky to travel with the group. I had the opportunity to speak with them at a more personal level which enabled me to be more ready to serve my country even better. We were picked up by a special hire, which one of them had arranged.

Juba was a sight. As we drove, we were greeted by so many empty polythene bags and plastic water bottles scattered all over the roads. Then we saw flies. At first it was not clear what the flies were hunting for, but soon we saw everything. We held our breath and looked away. As we reached *Jamia Juba* - The University of Juba—the sight of faeces on the road was too much for us. When we commented, the special hire driver said that was a normal sight they were used to. He did not explain why it was so.

The special hire took us to the home of Grace's brother, Akuu, who lived in Nimra Talata. We were received with great joy and ululations by the family of Datiro. We were happy to bathe in South Sudan's water, and eat food from South Sudan. We were finally home. So many neighbours came to see us and we had such a wonderful time throughout the day till evening. We were all glad to see each other alive. People shared their terrible experiences of war. So many people had been killed through the years. Mixed feelings settled in our midst. We thanked God and prayed that such scenarios should never again befall our country and we all said: *Insha Allah*.

That night the heat was so much that we decided to sleep outside. This was a new reality, so different from the cold of Nairobi. The mosquitoes too were too many but we put up the mosquito nets we had travelled with. We had been warned about the mosquitoes.

In the morning we went to see Grace's uncle who had lived in Juba since the 1950s. All wars came and left him in Juba. He was a living encyclopaedia of Sudan. He told us a lot of stories about the war and how he and all others who stayed had survived during bombing and burning of entire villages and through famine. We learnt a lot from him. This was a new day, a new beginning.

On Monday, only a few days after I arrived in Juba, I reported at my new workplace in the Ministry of Animal Resources and Fisheries in *Wizaharat*—where all the ministry offices were. For the time being, I put aside my plan to open a shop. After my graduation from Nkumba University, Kampala, in 2004, I had gone to Nairobi to apply for jobs in Juba. The headquarters of most international NGOs were in Nairobi and this was around the time when the peace talks about the war in the Sudan were almost coming to an end. I had been an active SPLM-A member as a student and so I had been following most of the discussions. That was my added advantage. In addition, my father Thomas Perembata had been a very instrumental chief, mobilising people in Madoro village to contribute food for the soldiers throughout the war period. Our home was a resting point for all the soldiers who would be passing through the village. So while in Nairobi submitting applications for jobs, I went for a Christmas party in the home of one of the prominent politicians from Southern Sudan. Many Zandes and other southern Sudanese communities were invited. We all introduced ourselves. When I mentioned my father's name, one of the politicians from my village who had already been appointed a minster called me and said he wanted me to go and work with him in Juba. He said that my father had been their great leader and he would be happy to work with me.

"If you are as hardworking as your father, I am sure you will be of help to the new establishment," he said.

"I will do my best if you give me the job," I replied.

"You will certainly. And did you say you are already a graduate?" he asked.

"Yes I am," I said. "I will bring you my papers tomorrow."

The following morning I had taken him all my papers. It was not until I returned to Juba that I knew he was serious. That is how I got my first job.

After settling down in Juba, I decided to go and visit my mother's grave. I had left my home for Uganda in December 1993 when my mother was alive and well. We used to sleep on the same bed. The day I left home, she said to me, "You must study hard my daughter in order to secure your future. It will only be a few years and you will be back with us." Leaving her was a time full of sadness.

Later I was joyful too as we flew from Entebbe International airport. Everything looked spectacular as this was my first time to leave my country and to fly. We were three girls Flora, Monica and I, and the pilot of Mission Fellowship Aviation (MAF). We were among the first students and girls to come from a liberated area to study in Uganda. This was a blessing to both our parents and the SPLAM leadership.

We had looked forward to a time when we would join our parents back home. Unfortunately my mother died in 2004 in the heat of war and I never got to know. By then we had no access to email, internet and telephone. Even letters could not be sent then. In 1997 when I heard about the death, I just wept and mourned for several days but still could not go since Sudan was still engulfed in war.

This was now 2006 when I finally went to her grave. Luckily, many relatives and friends gathered to mourn my mother with me. We worked on the grave and tiled it. It was the first grave to be built with tiles in Mariagba village in Ezo County. I stayed for a month before returning to Juba to resume for work.

The Ministry of Animal Resources and Fisheries, where I worked, shared an old building with the Ministry of Agriculture and Forestry. Most of the buildings in Juba had been destroyed. We were beginning from zero, but we were happy to make our contribution to rebuilding our country. Our ministry had few office spaces. Thank God I was taken to work as Executive Director in the minister's office. That meant that at least I had a place to sit and a table to work from. Some of my colleagues had neither office nor table. They would just come and hang around, sign the attendance book, do the work that needed to be done, and then go home. We had one computer that we all shared. Accomplishing tasks was hard because of the minimal resources but people did their best. We were also confronted by a stench from bats faeces. The ministry was located in an old colonial building which seemed to have become home to all the bats of Juba.

When it came to moving around Juba town, we walked because there was no public transport for most parts of the city. We all walked to work for almost three months, but we never complained. What mattered at the time was that we were back home and we were all struggling to make our contribution.

Finally, ministry vehicles arrived and as a director, I was among the first people to be given a ministry car with a Government of Southern Sudan (GOSS) number plate. This eased my movements and enabled me to accomplish my office tasks much more easily. Since I drove myself, I parked the car at my house in Munuki, the suburb where I lived.

Transport was now one challenge solved. But I had a host of other challenges that could not be solved overnight. I had left Sudan as a young girl and studied in Kenya and Uganda, where the official language is English. But the language spoken in Southern Sudan was Juba Arabic. It was difficult for me to communicate with most people and they did not bother with me since I did not know Arabic. The solution was one: I had to learn the language. In a few days, I started learning Juba Arabic. After about two months, I was able to speak it almost fluently. I was happy with myself and I began to enjoy my work and settle down.

One day, a group of four soldiers arrived at our office and stood on the office veranda. They were tall, dark, stick-like thin, and red-eyed. They had a lot of dust on their shoes and were all dressed in army green uniforms. They all held guns in their hands. People whispered that that was the habit with Juba soldiers, to carry their guns and move from one ministry to another demanding whatever they wanted. On that day the temperature was between 45 55 degrees Celsius. The heat was unbearable. Juba can really be hot. The men came at about noon, when the sun was at its hottest. Ministry staff served them water and they went away. By then it was clear that soldiers walked around demanding water or soda due to the heat of Juba but also because they had nothing to sustain themselves. That same day in the afternoon, a different group of soldiers arrived. I was in a meeting with members of the Multi-Donor Trust Fund about the animal sector.

I was busy contributing to the discussion when I heard someone running and making an alarm. It was our cleaner Jackline. She ran into my office where the meeting was taking place and we all stood up. She swung and locked the door behind her. She kept shouting, "We are dead! We are dead. Save us people!" We all swung into action and secured all the windows. The soldiers said they would not leave until they killed us. They were shouting and saying that since they were the ones who fought the war, who were we to refuse to give them water? They were wild with thirst. In Juba, thirst can kill and thirst can get one killed.

The men refused to move. They looked like they were ready to shoot. We stayed locked up inside the offices until we realized this was beyond us. We decided to call the police to come in and rescue us. When police arrived, they disarmed all of the soldiers, arrested them and took them to jail. They did not resist arrest. A week later we went and asked police to release them. They were suspended for six months after which they were called back. They were taken for some additional training and were later transferred from the army and integrated into the police force. Forces at different fronts were being trained to manage change.

I started to enjoy my work and learnt quite a lot. I mixed with other people in government and learned a lot from them. Everybody was ready to mentor and be mentored and I took every opportunity.

One evening at about 5pm, I drove home and decided to rest. It had been a long day of decision-making, meetings, calls, and paperwork. At around 7:30pm when I had just woken up and was preparing to go for dinner, I heard people running outside my house. I wondered what the chaos was about, so I decided to tiptoe to the window and peep out. Before I reached the window, I heard someone speak.

"Don't run," he was saying. "I am not chasing after any of you and I am not mad. I only want the person responsible for this government car that I see in the compound."

"But she is not here," somebody responded.

"Do not worry. I will sit here and wait till he or she comes," he said.

When I heard him insist, I moved out, only to find the man was dressed in a military uniform. He was armed too. He had a grenade, a machine-gun, and a knife in his hands. I shook with fear, realizing why there had been a lot of commotion outside. He must have scared people. As soon as he saw me, he walked towards me.

"Sister," he called.

"Yes Sir," I answered almost in a whisper.

"Go to Salva and bring my wife and children now, or else, I will kill you," he said.

"Brother, let's talk about this," I said. I was imagining he was indeed some mad man.

"There is nothing to talk about. I want my wife and children."

"But I am not able to go to Salva at this time of the night, my brother."

The soldier continued talking. He said that Salva Kiir, the President of South Sudan, had taken his wife and children. He said that since he had seen the government car with the GOSS number plate in my compound, I would certainly know how to reach the President. He told me that if I refused to go and bring his wife, he would spray me with all the bullets he had on his body.

"I will not leave you until I have my wife," he said. At first I thought he was just drunk and did not know what he was talking about but when he insisted, I realized he was sober and he knew what he was talking about. I became more scared. I was not sure of what to do. The man stared at me without blinking. As I racked my head, one idea came into my mind: to drive with him and go to the bishop's house in Kator. I was not sure what the bishop would do for me, but that is what I did. I asked my nephew to come with me and we drove in silence until we arrived at the parish.

At the parish, the first priest we met said that we should go to Saint Joseph's. He came with us but he said I should drive the car since I had brought it that far. I was shaking and had hoped that the priest was going to drive us to St Joseph's. That was not to be. I continued with my burden and all the while the man with weapons was silent. When we arrived at St. Joseph's and the priests saw us, they asked us what it was we wanted from them. The man told them what he wanted but they said that they were not able to help. They told me to return him where I had got him. We had hoped that they would at least suggest that we pray together but none of them dared suggest it. When they insisted that I take him away I asked them to pray.

"Fathers, *yagima, ana fakir gal Abuna waid bi Sali lakini mafizor fakir kalamu bita salawat ana yahu kelimu.*[57] Let us pray please," I begged.

"Okay," They responded and one of them offered a very short prayer.

After the prayer, I told the man to get back in the car so that we go wherever he wanted us to go. He jumped back into the car and we started driving towards Kator. The man must have sympathised with me after the long drive together for he changed his mind.

"Sister *itaa sol kuish ahsa*,"[58] he said to me. "I will go to your house and pick my motorbike."

I was surprised at the sudden change in approach.

"Where's your motorbike?" I asked him.

"I left it at your house," he said. All along I had not even noticed that he had left a motorcycle at my house.

"Okay Sir," I said.

"I will go and sleep in a hotel," he added.

It was already 11pm. I returned the priest to Kator and we drove to my house in Munuki. The man had the grenade and bullets all over his body all the time. I was worried they could explode and kill us any time. I had to be strong and brave because in case of fear and panic, I could easily cause an accident and all

---

57   Really, I had thought one of you priests would say a prayer for us but it looks like not even one person has thought about prayers. I had to remind you!
58   My sister, you are a good person.

of us would die. I thought about the incident with the priests and wondered. I had hoped that one or two of them would offer to come with me, but none offered. I was shocked that they could leave me, a woman, to brave the night with the vicious soldier, though men always consider women weaker. At that moment they could not even pretend.

I stepped on the accelerator pedal and held the driving wheel with a new strength I did not know I possessed. In a short while, we had arrived at my house unharmed. When we got home he took his bike and left.

The following day I reported the case to police. They hunted for the man and arrested him. I did not know him, but I had taken note of his motorbike. That is what they used to trace him. I later learnt that he worked with the security team in the office of the president, and that due to domestic violence, his wife had been taken away from him and hidden where he did not know. In the fight over the wife, he had retaliated by killing three soldiers after which he ran away. He would come out only in the night to terrorise people. That was the man who had walked into my compound.

For many days and months I was not able to sleep well. I would dream of gunshots and shout in my sleep. Still, I was grateful that I was back home.

# My Sister's Keeper

# Letter to my daughters

*Nyankiir Nyandeng Chaat*

Come,
My daughters,
My little queens
Gather at my feet
Let me tell you our stories
Of how our roots were watered
Deep.
Come, let me teach you
How to draw from our wells,
How to not be shaken!

Come,
My dear daughters,
Let me teach you
How not to silence your voices,
How not to belittle your desires,
How to love your men and build with them,
This, our nation.
Come my goddesses of love,
My princesses of peace.
Come.

# South Sudanese Woman

*Juan Evalyn Mule*

South Sudanese woman,
You are a warrior,
Let nobody push you aside.
Let nobody deceive you.
You are the brave defender of your future,
Stand up and pen your legacy,
What others can do, you too can do.
Do not listen to distracting voices.
Do not slumber,
Step into light and fight your fears
Fight until your fears fear you.
You are,
The resilient rock of South Sudan.

# To Women

*Emma Kwaje*

Her trouble is our problem
Her children, ours too
Her cry brings us to tears
Her joy makes us smile
No woman is pain-free
When one woman is in pain.

Let's stick together like a flock of birds
We shall not hunt for wind
Truth shall prevail
Let not anger seize our opportunity
To search for peace
In our hearts
Together
For the nation
For generation to generation.

The break of dawn
Sets my heart free
As the sun rises
My eyes start to see
The beauty of nature
An image of our future
Not far away from now
You cannot imagine
How hopeless darkness is without light
Let us make our own.

# A Poem for When my Sister Forgets,

*Piath Noi*

You are worth more than gold,
You have a temple enclosed within you.
You are multi-faceted;
Beautiful in the physical
Beautiful in the mind
Beautiful in the spiritual.

You are abundant in love, in care, in strength.
You are the gift that keeps on giving.
You are The Creator's proud creation,
A masterpiece to behold.
You were planned, considered and loved.

Moulded in purpose and deliberate precision.
You are no accident,
You are so much.
You are from God, of God
You make sense.

# My Sister's Keeper

*Julia Akur Magot*

I am a lawyer by training. Certainly, there is much more to me than my professional identity. There was a time when my career and professional identity mattered most over and above everything else. For a long time, my career was everything to me. I always unapologetically want to realize my maximum potential. I want to go to the grave empty, having expended all my talents and abilities. But like many other women, there have been times in my life when I have had to take time off from my career to perform care duties as a mother and wife. I have come to appreciate that life is not just about how much I make, chasing a career, and trying to get to the top of the ladder in record time, but also about how best I live for truth and how much love I give to those around me.

Sadly, coming from a country with a long history of conflict and growing up during the war that has lasted way into my adult life, I could not comfortably have both career and family without sacrificing one for the other. The war meant that my husband and I would live and work in South Sudan while our children lived and schooled in Kenya so they could access a good formal education. There was a time when we decided to put them into one of the schools in Juba, but at the sudden outset of the 2013 conflict, we relocated them back. This has been the painful reality for a number of South Sudanese families.

But we must not give up. As a lawyer I have been fortunate to work in a number of different sectors: humanitarian, development and government. I have had the opportunity to participate in the negotiation of multi-million dollar infrastructure projects, and to be part of high stakes arbitration proceedings in dynamic capital cities such as London, New York, Paris and Geneva. I have had the opportunity to work in male dominated sectors such as the petroleum sector. Sometimes I have been the only woman in the negotiations and meeting halls, even where western foreign investors were involved.

For me and for many other women, encouragement, affirmation and support are important, as we negotiate the many hurdles we face along our professional journeys.

My heart and soul beats for women's empowerment and rights, for the equal worth and dignity of women. Am I a feminist? I started off my earlier career days as a self- identified proud feminist. I had my own little manifesto as to why all women should become feminists. Imagine, Jewish men say in their prayers. 'Thank you God for not making me a woman!' The thought still outrages me! How dare they? So I started off identifying with the strain of difference feminism. To me difference feminism is probably the most radical of all as it posits that women have an alternative standard to that of men; an alternative voice of care. This difference school of thought on feminism which I ascribed to did not always sit very well with some women feminists, who leaned more towards liberal or radical feminism and who probably thought my approach was more of 'feminism light.' Others may have thought of me as downright disempowered or worse still a sell-out to the women's movement. But what does it matter as long as we are all working towards the liberation and empowerment of women?

I recollect the lessons I learned as a young law student from one of the first law reform exercises I participated in. It was at the Secretariat of Legal Affairs, one of the arms of the Civil Authority of the New Sudan. The Secretariat was established under the 1994 SPLM National Convention Resolutions to draft laws for the New Sudan to support civilian governance of the liberated areas under SPLA control. The drafting committee was comprised of only men and they drafted a number of New Sudan laws. In response to the absence of women in the drafting committee and the need to ensure that the laws were gender sensitive, the then New Sudan Women Federation convened a meeting of women to deliberate on these laws and formulate recommendations to be presented before the drafting committee. As a law student who had at the time just completed a semester on gender and the law, I was fortunate to participate in the deliberations of the women and to be part of the delegation that travelled to Rumbek where the New Sudan Judiciary was located and where the drafting committee was undertaking its work. I was all fired up and thought I had all the answers to women's disenfranchisement. We were equipped with theories and recommendations for sealing the gender gaps.

Unfortunately the meeting with the committee did not go very well and many of our recommendations were not readily taken on. We had several recommendations: abolition of the death penalty, registration of land to ensure women's land and inheritance rights were protected, ending child marriage, and much more. In protest we decided to boycott the meetings until the men were ready to take on board our recommendations. To our utter shock, the drafting committee proceeded in our absence and quickly reviewed and passed many of the laws.

From that experience, I decided I would always choose dialogue to try and talk to the hearts and minds of the 'opposition' as opposed to boycotting. So if I go into a controversial meeting and the men insist on calling me 'my daughter,' however patronising that is, I will answer 'yes Baba,' all the way until I get my view taken on board. Sometimes it is religion that is used to encourage inequality. But we should not waver in our quest.

Fast forward, at some point in my mid-career I got a chance to meet with a childhood role model who had initiated and played an active role in the development of the Sexual Offences Act of a neighbouring country. We invited her to South Sudan to share with South Sudanese female legislators, lawyers and members of civil society, the experiences and lessons learned from the development of their Act. Growing up, I had watched her on TV. Her confidence and boldness was captivating. Not to mention her bold hairstyles that sometimes ranged from bright red to a mohawk. I still promise myself that I will, one day, wear one of those bold hairstyles. It is on my to-do list. The meeting was a smash with all her first-hand experience both technical in terms of what such a law should look like as well as just practical in terms of getting male buy in and building alliances.

In one story she told us about a sexual harassment case that went to court and a male judge ruled in favour of the man accused of harassment for touching a woman's buttocks. The judge said the man was not guilty of breaking any law because buttocks do not amount to private parts! The women lawyers plotted a demonstration to storm court during one of the judges' sittings and then turn to his honour and bend showing him their buttocks since he did not, after all, consider buttocks as private parts. They however never executed their planned demonstration. Probably they feared they might end up in the cells for contempt of court.

Such women, whatever schools of thought they ascribe to, show us that what is important is belief in the equal worth and dignity of both men and women and that not a single feminist approach can work alone to eliminate inequality.

I have come to care so much about women's equality and empowerment because I grew up experiencing gender-based violence from the community around me – numerous incidents that left me wounded. They say time heals, but sometimes it just buries the pain we fear to confront. As a child, I grew up mostly around university campuses in Kenya. I recall one incident vividly.

When I was around 12 years old, my mother sent me to a dairy farm close-by to pick up the day's milk ration. As a child, I cherished being sent for the milk as it was an opportunity to get away from the house for a long period of time, lingering on the way there or back, under the pretext that the milk delivery had been late or that the line was too long.

This particular day, as usual, instead of going straight to the milk collection point, I first went off on my own escapades and headed to the market where women cheerfully chatted with each other at their small stalls. I went to play with their children in the market. Life can be so awesome as a child and you lose track of time. When I was finally on my way to the farm, which was located in a somewhat bushy and remote area, I came face to face with a drunkard. He was speaking profanities and commanding me to obey him. He staggered towards me and grabbed my arm and started to pull me saying he was going to rape me. I froze. Luckily for me, his slightly more sober friend was a little distance behind him, and he caught up with him and began to pull him away. I was completely shaken by the event. Up to this day, I recall the incident almost as vividly as if it were yesterday. And in particular, I remember the eyes of the drunkard. What I saw in them looked like rage and hatred. I was a child he found walking on the road. I had not done anything to him. In his eyes I saw power, and I felt my vulnerability.

After I was rescued, I continued my way to the farm, but reached long after it had closed. I went home with no milk. To explain, I had to tell at least one truth: I went playing and the diary closed. I said absolutely nothing about the encounter with the drunkard. How could I? Surely, in the mind of a child, I must have deserved it, I told myself. Such bad things happen to bad girls like me who do not follow instructions and fetch the milk on time! Yet it was an attempted rape, an attack that shook me to the core.

Seven years later, I was a young adult in my first year of law school. My family lived on the premises of the same university campus. Every day, I would leave the house and cross the road to go for my lectures. On my way I would pass by minibuses and touts. Out of courtesy, I would, cheerfully say hallo to the touts because I wanted to be civil and kind. A day came when the university students went on strike and the administration called in the riot police to quell the strike. I was not aware of the strike as it started when I was away. Later in the evening, I took a minibus from the town centre only to be dropped off at a bus stop about five kilometres from the main campus. Due to the strike, the minibus could not proceed into the campus. The university was located in a rural area. Many of the areas outside the main campus were not very developed or even well-lit with electricity. I decided to go and spend a night at the home of a former classmate who I knew lived in the vicinity. I started to navigate my way in the poorly lit area to my friend's house.

About one hundred metres away from where the minibus dropped us, I felt a hand grab me. The person begun to pull me towards the bushes while harshly commanding me not to make a noise. I was in complete shock. When I tried to see the person in the dim light, I could make out the features of one of the minibus touts I cheerfully greeted every day to and from university. I could tell it was him because he was wearing the same leather jacket that he always wore. I felt completely betrayed.

As he pulled me, I let out a very loud and piercing scream. In the shock of the moment he let go of my hand and shuffled away. I did not wait for any cue! I ran for dear life back to where I had left the other stranded passengers who were waiting for a solution. In due course I made it back home later that night as the buses were eventually allowed to go into the campus. But again, I said absolutely nothing to anyone at home about the incident. After all, I had survived it. But I kept asking myself: was it my fault because I was out at night and had even skipped my lectures? Surely if I had just been a good girl and had not skipped lectures I would have known about the strike? Was it something about the way I dressed that invited the attacks? Was it the way I behaved that made him want to harm me?

I felt like I was just a bad person and a magnet for such attacks. A number of female students were actually raped that night in the university during the chaos of the strike. The fact that I kept silent about my own ordeal continues to haunt me to this day. Surely, as a lawyer in the making, I should have known better than to just remain silent. I was haunted. What kind of lawyer would I possibly ever make? Did the man who attempted to rape me go on to rape another female student that night? But what could I have possibly said? What evidence did I have? How could I explain that I could without a doubt identify him even in the semi-darkness?

*No Time to Mourn*

It was not until much later as a young mother and after studying human rights and gender that I was actually able to name my own past experiences as violence and attempted rape. It was not until many, many years later, while seated in my pastor's office, that I was able to acknowledge the impact of the violence on my entire life and forgive myself for what was never my fault in the first place. Violence against women is so widespread and pervasive and one of the most tolerated forms of human rights violations. Because of the pervasiveness of the violence that women experience on an everyday basis, sadly it is considered normal. In my own case, I had come to blame myself for the violence that I had experienced.

My heart bleeds for women and girls who have been through an actual rape experience. I cannot even begin to imagine their pain and trauma. How does a good God allow such things to happen to good girls or even 'bad' girls, yet he promises to get us through every situation and turn it around for good.

For women who have experienced sexual violence, I want to take your hand and cry with you and offer you so much more than just the fine print of the law, and if the law fails us both, I offer you sisterhood.

I want to walk with women the day when they will learn that there is no shame in their stories, that past wounds do not define them and that what happened to them was no fault of theirs. That will truly be our day of victory.

I will be my sister's keeper. Will you?

# The Contributors

**Abai Hellen Mayom**'s life journey started in a rural environment in South Sudan. She writes to correct stories and impressions of her community and to contribute to a body of valuable reference material for men, women and children of South Sudan. Her work brings out the unrecognised potential of the woman. She just released her autobiography; *Struggles and Hope of an African Woman*.

**Grace Aben Kuol** is in medical school at Ahfad University for Women, in Khartoum, Sudan. She is passionate about true-life stories and documentaries as a means to exploring the world and unveiling the truth of her life and other lives around her. She is a happy woman and loves fun-filled company. Writing is her passion.

**Abul Oyay** lives in South Sudan. Her work shows the dynamics of conflict in South Sudan, which she lived through as a child. She credits her artistic influence to her early years spent with her paternal grandmother who practiced traditional arts and crafts. She has held exhibitions in the US, UK, South Sudan, Uganda and Kenya. Abul is a founding member of Anataban, a collective of youth creatives in South Sudan who use their art as a platform to demand peace and justice in the country.

**Grace Akon** is a first-generation South Sudanese American Poet. Her work explores a multitude of subjects, with a beautiful honesty. She fights for people like herself; those who feel tired of rearranging their words to make other people comfortable. Her work speaks to people who have been taught to be silent about their struggles, whether they are born from family, society, or religion. Grace has performed at several colleges and universities around the United States, as well as at The Loft Literary Center, one of the country's leading literary arts centers. She has been featured on *Button Poetry*, the largest distributor of spoken word poetry in the world. Grace also serves as a junior counsellor at *Slam Camp*, an annual writing and performance poetry intensive for high school students.

**Julia Akur Magot** is a lawyer by training but there is much more to her than her professional identity. Like many other women, she has had situations in her life where she has had to take time off her career to perform care roles as a mother and wife. It is during such times that she tries her hand at the creative pursuit of writing.

**Alith Cyer Mayar Cyerdit** is a social entrepreneur, the author of *The Cry of the South Sudanese Children* and *The Battle within Me*. She is founder of the Writers Fellowship in Juba and is currently the Director of External Relations at Starford International University.

**Monica Animbue** was born in 1996 in Yambio, Western Equatoria state. She went to Yabongo girls primary school in Yambio, Adu primary school in Maridi and Anyafio primary school in Arua. However, she could not advance further as per her story. She is now an Urban Refugee living in Kampala with her husband and three children.

**Apeay Ogeli** is a poet, Content creator, mentor, refugee advocate, youth program specialist for Refugees and At-risk Youth, based in San Diego, California. She is driven by the desire to impact lives positively by creating a safe space through representation in the workforce. She writes poetry to create a body of art that represents who she is and the self-development journey all humans go through.

**Atong Atem** is an artist and writer from Bor, living in Narrm, Melbourne. She is one of the first Africans to have their work acquired in 2019 as a permanent part of the National Victorian Gallery, Australian Collection.

**Emmanuella Baker Ayul** is a daughter of South Sudanese parents. As a young writer, she explores the art of poetry and creative writing as a tool into the human mind, emotion and feelings. She is still learning and finding her voice in the world through writing.

**Veoulla Baker Ayul** is a South Sudanese Australian young poet. She is a first year university student based in Melbourne. She was borne in Sudan but was raised, since the age of three, in Australia. She started writing songs from age eight and through her love of music and writing, she discovered poetry. She had her first performance at age seventeen.

**Bigoa Chol** is a writer and curator living on the lands of the Wurundjeri people of the Kulin Nation in Australia. She is the founder and Creative Director of Dichōtomi Magazine, an African diaspora art and literature publication. Bigoa writes in Thok Naath and English.

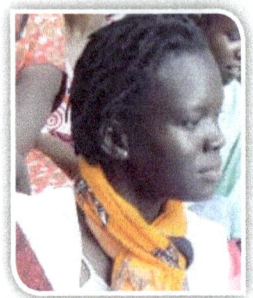

**Layet Busena** is a teacher by profession. She has lived outside South Sudan since she was a child, but always looks forward to a time South Sudan will be home to all her children who are currently scattered across the world.

**Chol Gatkek Tut** holds a master of international relations and a bachelor of conflict resolution and peace building from Kampala International University (KIU). She has wide experience in development work. She has worked on peace-building projects with A.C.O.R.D and has recently worked to provide information, counseling and legal assistance services to South Sudanese refugees living in Ethiopia. She is an advocate for women's participation in peacebuilding.

**Chudier Pelpel** lives in San Diego, California. She currently resides in San Francisco where she is a fulltime student in an undergraduate computer science program. She has been writing recreationally since she was 14 years, on topics of social stigma, culture and gender.

**Degineyo Flavia** was born in 2000 in Juba. She studied at White Angels Primary School and Naalya Secondary School in Uganda. She is currently doing her bachelors of laws at the Catholic University of Eastern Africa in Kenya. She is very passionate about art because it impacts and empowers hearts.

**Emmanuela Erasto** is an independent senior reporter with Almaugif newspaper. She is a proactive writer, open to new ideas, curious and willing to learn. She is a peace activist, an adventurer, a radio presenter, translator, news anchor and a dancer. She is interested in documentation and empowering people with the right information on how to protect themselves and change their attitude and lifestyle for the better.

**Mary Kadi** is a writer who has featured as a story teller in a virtual global women's movement which uses local voices and story-telling to build awareness about gender-based violence, migration, security, health and other issues of concern. She is also interested in film and documentaries as a strategy to stimulate conversations. She is determined to use her writing skills to contribute to South Sudan literary memory.

**Kaka** is a poet and creative writer living in Melbourne, Australia. She writes to make life relatable.

**Kiden Jackline** uses her pen to document issues of social justice. She still writes under pen name but hopes that a day will soon come when she will be able to tell her stories publicly and without fear.

**Lucy Kiden Lulu** is many things. She is a creative writer, an administrator, a journalist, an events coordinator and moderator, a vocalist, a content creator, and a script and song writer.

**Emma Kwaje** holds a secondary school certificate and is pursuing a degree in mass communication, from the University of Juba. She is a presenter with a children's radio program - Sama FM 99.3. She has also worked as a rural peace ambassador with Okay Africa foundation (OAF), a Gospel singer and a BBC Media Action freelance actress for "Life in Lulu" Radio drama. She is volunteering for the Reproductive Health Association of South Sudan (RHASS) as an executive member of Youth Action Movement (YAM).

**Mare Lodu** is an interdisciplinary artist, writer and aspiring archivist. She studied art history at the University of Minnesota. Her work incorporates historical research, archival practices and image-making to explore and interrogate the legacies of colonialism and the global struggle for Black liberation.

**Maree Nikimaya** is a young artist living in Tasmania. To her, art perfectly represents culture, nature and femininity, which are the three main vessels of inspiration for all her artworks. She hopes to continue displaying her understanding of culture, nature and femininity in her artwork for the rest of her life.

**Lydia Minagano Kape** studied at School of public service, University of juba and Cavendish University in Uganda. She is an activist, a writer and a co-founder of Heroines Unspoken Tales, **an initiative** that amplifies women's voices and stories through writing and storytelling. Some of her poems were featured in the Ana Taban's youth poetet anthology, *Soutna* in 2017. Her new obsessions include chasing the sunsets, watching darkness turn to light and speaking to the Nile.

**Juan Evalyn Mule** was born in 1998 to the late Samuel Mule Enoka and Mrs Lucy Sokale Mule in Kajokeji County in the Central Equatoria state. She attended St. Daniel Comboni and Mirembe primary school, Mukono. She later joined Bishop's Senior School Mukono for both her ordinary and advanced level. She is currently in her final Semester at Ndejje University pursuing bachelors in journalism and mass communication.

**Winnie Elijah Musomba** is a writer and performer who believes in being and doing the best she can. She lives between Juba, Kampala and Nairobi. Her book, *Rituals of a Full House* was published on Amazon in 2018. Her love for writing started way back and I started writing short stories for children in the South Sudan Mirror in Kenya.

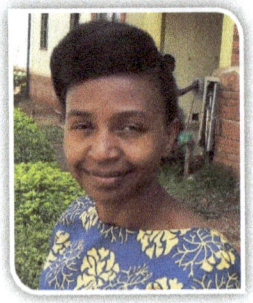

**Charity Naume Naigupai** was born in Yambio to Rev. Charles Bangbe and Jane Michael Pia. She is a survivor of the civil war. She writes to bring to light the plight of women and girls during war. She is a lawyer and has served her country as a Girl's Education Campaign leader. She is a legal drafter and works with humanitarian organisations to sensitise returnees and internally displaced persons on laws of South Sudan. She lives in Juba with her husband Paul Lado Reuben and their two daughters Isabella Yatet and Abigail Busan.

**Piath Noi** was raised in Australia. Although she left Sudan as an infant, her memories of conflict and displacement are not forgotten. Like many young refugees, she carries these memories and they keep returning as she battles the challenge to understand and reconcile her identity, womanhood and belonging, to the new land where she now lives. These memories have inspired the internal conversations and dreams that she depicts in the poems she is sharing for the first time.

*No Time to Mourn*

**Nyakoda Joak Mundit** is a feminist and women rights activist. She has worked with different organizations and coalitions on Gender-related issues. She is a former senior Inspector for Girls Education South Sudan and currently works as a Program officer for National Education Coalition, an advocate for child protection and safeguarding.

**Theresa Nyalony Gatwang** is a believer in love, truth and honesty. She lives in Juba. She writes poetry and short stories to find meaning in life.

**Nyankiir Nyandeng Chaat** is a peace builder and community developer. She holds a master's degree in diplomacy, development and international relations from Daystar University in Kenya. She works with Girls Education South Sudan (GESS) as a full time academic researcher. She is a poet and a creative writer and is part of the South Sudanese women writers for peace team.

**Nyareeta Gach** is a poet and aspiring gallerist fervent, in her desires as a professional artist. Born in Maiwut, Sudan in 1992 during the nation's second civil war, she left home with her family to seek sanctuary in Ethiopia when she was only nine-months-old. Her family later found asylum in Hagadera Refugee camp in the town of Dadaab, Kenya, where she spent most of her childhood. In 2001, the family immigrated to the United States where she grew up in central Minnesota. In 2010, Nyareeta joined the Rocky Mountain College of Art and Design and began her study in fine arts with an emphasis on painting. The ambitious young artist currently lives in New York City where she exhibits and continues her art practice.

**Ruth Nyaruot Ruach** is a cultural curator, multidisciplinary artist, who uses art to heal, explore her surroundings and create comfort within her blackness. Ruth's art explores the experiences of being an African of the diaspora. She is strongly influenced by decolonising language, tone, and the cultivation of shared perspectives in place of assimilation.

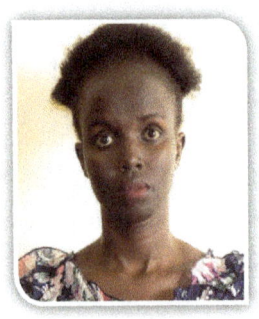

**Nyibol Ajang Adier** is an industrious medical student and a writer with so much love for saving lives through her skills. She hopes to become a surgeon one day. She was born in 1996 during the war of liberation in the Sudan, the present day republic of South Sudan. Her father was a freedom fighter. Her grandfather, Solomon Adier Deng was also one of the commanders of Anyanya one war. She has had all her education in Uganda where she is currently studying medicine at university. She writes and bakes to support her education and skills development.

**Susan Thomas Perembata** is a graduated with a Bachelor's degree in business administration and Management from Nkumba University in Uganda. She has attended various intensive trainings in gender equality and peace building in several Asian and African countries.

*No Time to Mourn*

Currently, Perembata is the Chairperson of the Women's Network for Peace Building. She is an active member of South Sudanese Women Writers group.

**Hellena Rial Isaac Nyariel** was born in 1996. She studied at Comboni primary school, Mapuordit in South Sudan, Loreto Girls Secondary School in Burundi and is currently at Tangaza University College in Langata Kenya, studying social transformation.

**Sunday Makuach** is a versatile artist, who is eager to learn and create through different styles and mediums including graphite drawing, traditional painting, digital illustration, textiles and murals. Sunday values the freedom of exploring the experiences of young South Sudanese women living in Australia. Through her multifaceted visual arts, she contemplates the interconnectedness of belonging, self-acceptance, culture and identity. She hopes others can relate to her visual representations of some of those lived realities.

**Suzan Voga Duffee** is a professional with 13 years of work experience in the education, development and humanitarian response sectors as a teacher, educationist, trainer, mentor and coach. She holds a master of research degree in international education and development and a bachelor's degree in English and literature. She is currently an independent consultant in the areas of education, training, resource mobilisation and development. Her desire is to write so that someday she is able to join the ranks of Maya Angelou and be counted among great African writers.

**Vonda Keji** is a visual artist living in Melbourne, Australia. She is a painter, an illustrator and photographer. Her works utilise surrealism, colours, symbolism and social issues to aver the beauty and complexity of her African identity in addition to speaking on issues that affect the African diaspora. She's heavily influenced by the political motivation of the black arts movements. Through her work she seeks to breakdown society's misconceptions.

**Grace Wenepai Enosa (Apostle)** was born in South Sudan. Her father Enosa Mbaraza was a pastor. She is a single mother to five children. In 2003, she was resettled to Norway where she founded Jesus International Evangelical Ministry in 2008. She has a strong relationship with God due to her encounter with the supernatural power of God one night in 2001. She has experienced God's presence and heard His voice in times of extreme suffering. She is passionate about helping other people. She is a prayerful woman with a passion to preach the gospel.

# Editors

**Elizabeth Ashamu Deng** is a human rights lawyer currently leading Oxfam's humanitarian advocacy in the Horn, East and Central Africa. She previously worked with Amnesty International and Human Rights Watch conducting research on the human rights situation in South Sudan. She is committed to supporting people affected by conflict and crises, particularly women and refugees, to actively participate in addressing the challenges they confront. She holds Bachelor's and Master's degrees in African Studies from Yale University and a Juris Doctoris (JD) degree from New York University School of Law.

**Hilda J. Twongyeirwe** is a feminist, presently the Executive Director of FEMRITE – Uganda Women Writers Association. Her poem: Threshold, introduces a section in Mire Soraya's memoir against Female Genital Mutilation; The Girl with Three Legs. Twongyeirwe has coordinated various writing and editorial activities with FEMRITE, Action for Development (ACFODE), the MGLSD Uganda Woman Magazine, African Women Development Fund and Oxfam. She was awarded: a National Medal of the Government of Uganda, the Women for Women – Uganda Award 2018 and the Uganda Registration Services Bureau Award 2018, for her commitment to women emancipation through Literary Arts. She holds a Bachelor's degree in social sciences, a master's in public administration and management and a diploma in education.